GURUDEV

ON THE PLATEAU OF THE PEAK

GURUDEV

ON THE PLATEAU OF THE PEAK

THE LIFE OF SRI SRI RAVI SHANKAR

BHANUMATHI NARASIMHAN

Published by Westland Publications Private Limited
61, 2nd Floor, Silverline Building, Alapakkam Main Road,
Maduravoyal, Chennai 600095

Westland and the Westland logo are trademarks of
Westland Publications Private Limited, or its affiliates.

Text Copyright © Bhanumathi Narasimhan 2018
Images Copyright © Art of Living 2018

ISBN: 9789386850577

Typeset in Garamond Premier Pro by SÜRYA, New Delhi
Printed at Thomson Press (India) Ltd.

Providence has laid down the track for the journey to infinity,
as many await ...

CONTENTS

PROLOGUE

TRUTH IS MULTIDIMENSIONAL.

Seated in the front row of a press conference organized in the ballroom of Hotel Nacional de Cuba, I felt like an island of calmness amidst a storm of emotions and unanswered questions hanging in the air. In the room, at least a hundred different conversations buzzed in Spanish. The floor was covered with a web of video camera cables of scores of TV stations. The cameramen kept shuffling around, trying to make sure they had the best vantage point. Most of them were unprepared for the truth of that moment. Ivan Marquez, the leader of the Revolutionary Armed Forces of Colombia—People's Army (FARC), walked in and took a seat, followed by Gurudev. Dressed in gleaming white robes, with his long hair and beard, Gurudev's saintly appearance was in sharp contrast to the general dress code of the place. Suddenly, all attention was focused on the stage. 'We agree with Master Shankar,' said Ivan Marquez, 'that deep down, we are all victims. And if we begin with that understanding, we can leave behind the past, a sad story of violence that must not be repeated. With his help, we place our spirit in reconciliation with and in coexistence with our benevolent country, whose destiny cannot be that of war. We can have our political goals but with a new vision of non-violence.'

Responsible for the loss of nearly 250,000 lives over a period of fifty years, it was true that many looked at the FARC members as criminals. Yet, in Gurudev's eyes, it was also true that they were victims crying for help. These men of war, deep inside, sought a better future for their children. This was not the first time that Gurudev was taking up a cause like this. Driving into the red zone of Iraq, where even UN personnel think twice before venturing; walking through the 'No man's land' in Sri Lanka in an effort to reach out to the LTTE; visiting a war-torn Ukraine to revive its people's hope—was there anything that my brother would not do for peace? This was the first time that I was accompanying him on such a mission.

On 25 June 2015, we arrived in Bogota, Colombia, on the invitation of President Juan Manuel Santos. A ten-minute private meeting with the president turned into an hour-long discussion, and Gurudev promised to do whatever it takes to chart out a peace agreement. As we left and were on our way to Havana, I thought we were going to be in agyaat—a few days of silence and rest. Little did I know what was in store for me. When we landed, we were picked up in a vintage car. I thought they had arranged it especially for Gurudev but soon realized that all cars in Cuba were similar.

The hotel was an old Victorian building—ornate, white, and clean. My room was spacious. In one corner was a study. The bedside lamps were pretty and hand-painted. I had a very pleasant feeling within me. I settled in and slept with the thought of the beautiful dawn that I would wake up to. The next day, there was excitement as everyone got ready for the meeting. Although I did not speak a word of Spanish, I said, 'I'm coming too!' I was told that there would be guerrilla leaders and got mentally prepared to meet fierce-looking men with extreme ideologies. But I was pleasantly surprised to meet highly educated people who, despite their tense exterior, exuded warmth and softness. Everyone was supposed to be unarmed, but I had a feeling that weapons were somewhere within their reach.

They spoke with a great level of involvement. The translator was trying to express their feelings, but a sense of fatigue and frustration was visible. They had lost so many of their own kith and kin; they were tired of waging a ceaseless war. There were a few women present as well, and I was told that about 40 per cent of FARC members were women. Many of the commanders were in their late fifties and sixties and the urgency for peace was very evident. They had their own press, TV station, and almost ran a parallel government. They were powerful, yet sought change. Gurudev listened to each one of them, shared their concerns, and deliberated together.

Every moment was poignant. On the very first day, a connection was made. On the second day, they recognized him as a Master. 'I have only seen wooden and stone figures of saints before, but today I stand before a living saint,' said Pastor Alape, one of the FARC commanders. He gave Gurudev two stones—one to be charged with his energy and returned to the FARC, so that their people may touch the stone and feel his presence; and the other for Gurudev to keep. On the third day, they held Gurudev's hand and said, 'We promise the Master that we will adopt the Gandhian principles of non-violence.' I was touched. How was this possible? After having lived their entire lives as per certain rigid systems, they had melted in a matter of three days. Gurudev had inspired valour in the principle of non-violence. One of the journalists wanted to know how Gurudev had managed to change the minds of the FARC members so drastically. But was it really what was said that mattered or *who* said it that made all the difference?

We tend to live in our own bubbles. But travelling with Gurudev allows me to break free of these bubbles as I see people waiting for him everywhere. For instance, we met some representatives of the Mexican parliament in the hotel elevator. Gurudev greeted them, and when they came to know that he had come for peace talks, they were delighted and invited him to address the parliament in Mexico. Colombia, South Africa or the North Pole, airports, railway stations or walkways, the truth is that people *are* waiting for him. I have accompanied him to ninety countries, and everywhere I experience the cry of hearts, the longing of sincere seekers, and the ultimate quest of intellects to connect to something higher. And I have seen this connection happen naturally for so many through him.

Media hailed it as a historic moment. I was privileged to watch it unfold in front of my very eyes. As a child, while walking along the shores of the ocean, I would collect seashells, so delicate and pretty, and would feel that each one was a precious treasure. Now, walking along the shores of time, I feel that I have collected many such precious moments in my life. We went for a stroll along the beach with Gurudev after the press meet. I walked in silence, enjoying the soothing sound of the ocean. So many events in my life have risen and dissolved like the waves in front of me. Yet, there is stillness in the ocean depths. Everything around me has changed, but I have remained the same. Gurudev has remained the same. Once again I pinch myself to make sure that it is true—he is my brother, my Master. But who in reality *is* he?

1

SUNRISE AT MIDNIGHT

A TINY DROPLET of water fell from the dark midnight sky on to the coconut leaves before touching the earth—a forerunner to the summer rains. A refreshing coolness spread through the veins of the thirsty soil as each drop made gentle contact in the secret of the night. The fragrance of the earth rose to fill the open courtyard as the rains showered upon it. Rains were auspicious, a sign that the devas (angels) were happy. A gentle smile crept upon Alamelu perima's (aunt's) face as she looked up to the heavens in acknowledgement. The attention of all the others was focused on the deep breaths and moans that escaped the solid teak doors of the small delivery room in my mother's parental home in Papanasam. Little did anyone know what a beautiful journey was about to begin.

My memories of Papanasam are of a sweet, simple village, peaceful yet vibrant with activity. Located about twenty-five kilometres from the city of Thanjavur in Tamil Nadu, its name means the 'destruction of sins'. Its dusty narrow streets were lined with rows of Chettinad-style houses with their typical verandahs and pillars. Elaborate designs made of rice powder called rangoli, displaying the creativity of the women of the house, decorated the entrance area leading up to the threshold. Small squirrels scurrying back and forth feasted on the rice powder, as did little rows of ants meticulously carrying it away grain by grain.

Our house, like most others in the village, was a long, single-storeyed structure with stone floors, a central courtyard, terracotta-tiled roof and lime-plastered walls with a triangular slot cut into it for the evening lamp. It was home to all the four brothers and three sisters of Amma's family. Alamelu perima was the eldest of the seven. All my uncles and aunts were thin, sharp-featured, of moderate height, 'wheatish' complexioned and spoke eloquent Tamil. They were a close-knit family and especially dear to Amma. The family of my grandfather's younger brother also lived there. Coming to Papanasam was coming home to all of them.

A narrow portico outside the house, 'thinnai', where most guests are entertained, led to the entrance double-door made of solid Burma teak with an intricately carved Lakshmi panel at its head. As one stepped in, the house opened out into a broad corridor hall lined with pillars, leading to individual rooms. Light streamed in, as did fresh air, through the open-to-the-sky courtyard. Beyond this hall was the kitchen, the dynamic centre of activity in the early mornings where the sounds of chopping, chanting, chatting resonated harmoniously. Mornings were busy at home with the arrival of Swaminathan, the caretaker of the paddy fields, the vegetable vendor with his baskets of fresh produce, and the flower vendor with the most exotic jasmine flowers strung together deftly on cool banana fibres and made into beautiful garlands. We performed puja every morning and visits to nearby temples were routine. Lunch was usually served on banana leaves and we sipped hot coffee while sitting and chatting together in the late afternoons. Carnatic classical music and veena in the open courtyard were part of the general evening routine.

Amma was from an orthodox Brahmin family deeply rooted in tradition and values. She had a religious temperament, was exceptionally meticulous in whatever she did, and had a balanced approach in catering to the diverse requirements of all the family members. Wearing a clean crisp sari, which she would carefully iron herself, and with her long hair tied up in a neat bun, she was the image of perfection for me. Amma used to say that one day she felt a beam of light entering her and she conceived soon after. In India, it is customary for a girl to be at her mother's home when she is pregnant. A few months into the pregnancy, while resting in the afternoon, she heard the voice of the child calling out to her saying, 'Amma, are you fine?' She immediately shared it with her elder sister. Alamelu perima felt that the way every mother could feel a child kicking in the womb when she was sensitive, perhaps it was possible to communicate with the child too! These women, though practical, had faith in all possibilities.

13 May 1956. The special day arrived, and my uncles, Perima, Paati (mother's mother) Seethalakshmi, Savithri atthaipaati (my grandfather's sister) and her family were all in the house. A small room (casually called the camera room where boxes and other household goods would be stored, like a utility room), to the right as one entered, was cleared out for the delivery of the baby. The midwife, whose name was Thangam, was called for assistance. The whole family waited with great excitement for Vishalam's baby.

Paati was inside the room with my mother, assisting the midwife. The uncles were pacing up and down, a little nervous and, of course, eagerly waiting as they watched Alamelu perima going in and out of the little room, which was the centre of all activity. 'The baby has a large head,' observed Thangam as she encouraged Vishalam to push a little more. The gentle pitter-patter of raindrops and the sounds of deep breathing mingled with the sound of Vedic chants that made its way into the house from a midnight procession of the deity from the nearby Shiva temple. When a deity from a temple passed by, it was common practice for household members to stand up and offer salutations. My uncles stepped out and as the Lord passed by the house, the little bundle of light and joy arrived. The entire family held their breath as the little one took its first breath and started crying. Alamelu perima, who was the first to hold the baby in her arms, felt a gentle stirring in her heart as she looked into the radiant dusky face and the abundant curly locks of the child. 'It's a boy,' she announced to the rest of the delighted family.

All the gods were thanked. They felt great pride and happiness in welcoming the little baby boy of their dearest sister. One of my uncles sent a telegram the next morning to my father who was in Bangalore. Trains were the fastest mode of transport those days. Pitaji boarded a train to Tiruchirapalli and took a bus from there to Papanasam. Though he was yet to see the baby, the time of his birth spoke volumes to my father.

Pitaji was a student of Vedic astrology and Ayurveda. He mapped out the child's horoscope and shared its uniqueness with other family members. Four planets were in exalted positions in addition to other very special configurations.

This gave him an inkling that the child's path would be extraordinary. The day of the baby's birth also coincided with the birth anniversaries of two great Indian saints and reformers, Sri Adi Shankara and Sri Ramanujacharya. Adi Shankara was the proponent of Advaita philosophy (monism) and Sri Ramanuja was the proponent of Vishishtadvaita philosophy (qualified monism) and was one of the most important saints of the Sri Vaishnava tradition. As our family had great respect for traditions and reverence for saints, it was a matter of celebration that the child's birthdate coincided with the anniversaries. This also certainly influenced the choice of the child's name.

My father's mother was a clairvoyant and had predicted long before that Pitaji would have a son and a daughter. 'He will bring light to the whole world. Name him Ravi,' she had said. 'Ravi' in Sanskrit means the sun, and coincidentally the day of the child's birth was a Sunday. She had also suggested that I be named 'Bhanu', which also means the sun. Honouring her words, 'Ravi' was decided as the name and 'Shankar' was added in reverence to Adi Shankara. They even had the idea of including 'Narayana' because of the Ramanuja connection but decided against it as 'Ravi Shankar Narayana' would be too long for a name. On the auspicious eleventh day of the baby's birth, the name 'Ravi Shankar' was whispered into his ears by my father.

A few more days passed by, and as was the routine, in the afternoons, Amma would rest with the baby in a room adjacent to the courtyard. One day, a warm glow filled the room. The baby was lying on a soft white cloth beside Amma. As she rose to investigate the source of the light, she had a vision of several saints blessing the child. A few months after this incident, the shankaracharya of Shivganga (in Karnataka) visited our house. Amma sought his blessings for the child. The shankaracharya saw the lovely face of the baby and noticed a special mark on his back. His eyes shone with joy as he said, 'You are lucky and blessed to be his mother.'

Later, Amma would say that the shankaracharya folded his hands in respect to the baby. This was an unexpected event for the young mother. Taking a child to saints to get their blessings is a common tradition in India. Even the most revered shankaracharyas from Sringeri and Kanchi recognized the divine spark in the child. While it was a matter of great joy to receive the attention of these revered souls, it certainly left some questions in my mother's mind as to what the future held for her son.

Pitaji, too, would often narrate a few incidents that reminded him of a divine presence protecting the child. Many village houses those days had heavy cradles, in which both the child and mother could sleep. The broad corridor hall of the house had one such wooden cradle tethered to a solid wooden beam with iron chains. One day, as Amma was rocking the baby to sleep, Pitaji arrived home. As she went to the door to receive him, the iron chains holding the cradle gave way and the cradle with the baby inside it crashed with a loud thud. Shocked, Amma fainted. As he saw the damaged cradle, Pitaji, holding Amma, feared for his child's life. However, he was filled with amazement when he discovered that the child was safe and in a playful mood inside the damaged cradle. The heavy iron chains had fallen outwards, defying the laws of physics. Alamelu perima rushed to the cradle, took the baby out and cried out loud, 'The boy is safe!' After some time, Amma regained her composure, and as she held the baby close to her she cried and laughed with tears of joy streaming down her face. 'God has saved our son,' she said as she handed over the baby to Pitaji trembling with tearful eyes.

On another occasion, my mother was travelling to the Swamimalai temple in a bullock cart with the baby. Her sisters, brother and his wife accompanied her. It was a ten-kilometre ride. Once they reached, they started alighting from the cart one by one. Amma was the last one to get out. As she picked up the baby from the cart, the wheel of the cart came unhinged and the whole cart collapsed. Later, we came to know that the pin of the wheel's axle had fallen off somewhere three kilometres back! Everyone was amazed. How did the bullock cart manage to stay together through the journey? Why did it collapse only after Amma had picked up the child? There was no logical explanation and the overwhelming emotion among everyone was of gratitude for the divine. My mother was anxious, but even as my father shared her concerns, he was fully aware that challenges were an inescapable part of one's life and perceived in the event signs of a higher power protecting their son.

2

IDLIS, COWS, TEMPLES AND GAMES

ONCE LITTLE RAVI was a few months old, Amma returned to Bangalore. Pitaji was working with the automobile industry and was involved in the development of fuel-efficient cars. Pitaji's mother, Shringaramma (we called her Atthaiamma), his brother Subramaniam and sister Vasantha lived with us. Our first house in Bangalore was a rented place in an area called Minerva Circle. Later, we moved into Manjula, our own little cozy house. Atthaiamma had chosen the name Manjula for our new house. She was a beautiful lady with a bright round face, long hair, a beaming smile and brilliant personality. When my father was in the process of buying a house, he had narrowed down two options in an area called Jayanagar in Bangalore, both located on the same street. One was a large corner house and the other was Manjula, which was relatively smaller. He discussed both the options with Atthaiamma who chose the smaller house saying, 'We can all be closer to each other in a smaller house. This is enough for us!' Her intuition was right. I would have been around four years when we moved into Manjula. This house was the stage for our precious growing years and has always been full with friends and relatives. Manjula exuded an atmosphere of warmth and homeliness. In contrast, the corner house has been rarely occupied in all these years. No one could stay there for long.

The area was full of trees and birds. We had mango, chiku, coconut and several other trees around the house. Pitaji would tell us that when my brother was a little over a year old, Amma would point out birds and other small animals in the garden for him. The animals would sing and play along with the swaying of the wind and the sun, and little Ravi would laugh and clap with wide-eyed interest.

Less than two years after little Ravi arrived, on 11 January 1958, I was born. This was the time of the Thyagaraja aradhana and most of the family, except for my mother and Paati, had gone to Thiruvaiyaru, a town about twenty kilometres away from Papanasam, to take part in the festivities. The family stayed at the house of a great musician there. However, by late afternoon, my mother began to experience labour pains. Paati rushed to the bus depot, found a bus that was going to Thiruvaiyaru, and sent a message with the driver, 'Tell them to come home immediately!' The driver went to the house of the musician and informed Alamelu perima about the news. Soon the whole family was back to Manjula, taking care of little Ravi and waiting for my arrival.

I was always very attached to my brother since I was a baby. My mother would tell me how even as he was just a year and a half, my brother was very caring towards me. Sometimes my aunts would tease him saying, 'Your sister looks like a doll, and the neighbours want her for themselves.' Then he would not allow any visitors to touch me and would watch over me gently. He would let his tiny finger into my baby hands and rejoice as my fingers curled around his.

Time flies when one is happy. When my brother was around four and I was about two, he started chanting and praying, much to the amazement of people. I would watch him and imitate his actions. When he was asked what it was he prayed for, he would say, 'for everyone to be happy'. We used to watch the clouds, the sky, the stars, the sun, the moon, and well ... pray to them all. He would pray with his eyes closed, and I with one eye closed and another open, watching out for his next move. They say old habits die hard. Even now I see him with eyes both closed or open. He is the one I pray to. He is pleased when one is prayerful.

Prayers happen spontaneously, and rituals associated with prayer add colour to our life. Lighting the little oil lamps, decorating the idols with flowers, the fragrant sandal paste, the bells ringing—these small activities create an atmosphere of sacredness and celebration for the whole family. Taking the kavadi, a sacred vow in reverence to Lord Subrahmanya, in the Swamimalai Subramanya temple was a special ritual for Amma during the summer. The temple was located on top of a small hill and she would carry a pot of milk on her head and circumambulate the temple sanctum. Amma would go into a trance-like state. My brother would walk with her gently, guiding her path, and I would walk along with them. As Amma walked with her eyes closed, milk would overflow from the pot and soak her sari. However, at the sanctum sanctorum, where we were to offer the milk as oblations to Lord Subramanya, the pot would still be full.

We would stay at Alamelu perima's house whenever we

went to Kumbakonam to visit the Swamimalai temple. Once a neighbour came to Perima's house with the news that a priest from the tradition of Sri Muthuswami Dikshithar, a great devotee of Lord Subramanya, had arrived. Amma, along with little Ravi, went to meet the priest to get his blessings. The priest was told that little Ravi would often sit in meditation even as a child. He wanted to give the boy a gift and entered the room with a silver bowl filled with different objects. He spread each one of the objects in front of my brother and asked him to pick whatever he liked. Without hesitation, little Ravi chose an emerald Shiva lingam and placed a silver naga on top of it. The priest jumped up in excitement, exclaiming 'I was waiting for this day!' Apparently, Sri Muthuswamy Dikshithar, an eighteenth-century poet and saint and a Carnatic music maestro, had spoken of a prophecy that the person who would re-establish dharma in the world would select the lingam and the naga. He asked me also to choose and I picked up a small silver Vishnu paada (image of the feet of Lord Vishnu). This incident provided further food for thought for my mother as she returned home after the meeting. Though many such predictions were being made, they would take a back seat soon after, and Amma, Perima and Paati would all go back to their regular lives, taking care of the two little children.

The occasional passerby on a bicycle, the intermittent temple bells from the Srinivasa Perumal temple, the incessant chirping of sparrows, the contented mooing of cows and their calves—these were the sights and sounds that characterized our day in the village. Within our home, the fragrance of freshly brewed coffee, piping hot idlis and steaming rasam rice with ghee awaited us. We had a small cowshed near our house, and my brother and I would go visit the calves at the cowshed and try talking to them. Little Ravi used to feel that the calves starved as we drank all their milk. So Paati would take us to the calves when they drank milk from their mother and tell us all about the food habits of cows. My brother loved the cows, and whenever he felt hungry, he would feed them as well. This was also part of our recreation. Children do not need special toys. Everything that they do is playful. As one grows older, intelligence dawns and matures into wisdom. And yet again, we start perceiving life as part of a divine play.

Our recreational schedule included visits to all the nearby temples. I would play with my cousin Hema, her brother Shankar, and a few other children from the neighbourhood. My brother was a natural leader and would decide what we should do next and how to go about it. At the Ganesha temple, he would make us all pull our ears and do sit-ups. This ancient practice is now known to help brain development and is called 'super-brain yoga' by some researchers. At the temple of Lord Srinivasa (Vishnu), the priest would place a crown upon our heads. The steps to the sanctum had stone railings that were perfect for comfortable slides. We had so much fun there, running up the steps to the sanctum and sliding down while laughing the whole time! In the Shiva temple, there were 108 Shivalingas. My brother would go around each one of them chanting 'Om Namah Shivaya'. I would follow him. His feet were small but mine were smaller. Occasionally, wanting to catch up with him, I would skip circumambulating a linga, but he would point it out and make me go around it. Now I wonder how he knew every time I skipped, but at that time, I just followed his instructions innocently.

My brother engaged me in all the games that he played. With his small hands he would mould a Shivalingam from the sand and mud that was abundant in the village. The shape would be perfect, and every particle of sand would stay where he had gently kept it. We gathered flowers, leaves, water and other materials for worship—Hema and I were his assistants, and together we would do a puja. The leaves and flowers were placed reverently and gracefully on the Shivalingam. He would not think about where a flower should go or how to arrange them. He would spontaneously place them one after the other. When he was done, it would be simple, beautiful and perfect. Little Ravi was the main pundit and we followed his instructions. He would say, 'Close your eyes and smile'—his favorite instruction before he started the puja.

One summer afternoon, one of our neighbours came home with the news that Ammalu amma, a woman saint, had arrived. She sang devotional songs in praise of Lord Krishna and people danced at her gathering. This was a very uncommon sight in the conservative south. So, out of curiosity, we went to her satsang. People were swaying with their hands raised above their heads, dancing gently, and singing '*Radhe Govinda ...*' led by the saint herself.

Once we came home, little Ravi took all of us (me, Hema, Shankar and the other neighbourhood kids) to the courtyard. We filled water in all the vessels that we could find, added sandal powder to the water, and threw in a few flowers and petals too. We filled the water in smaller containers, which became our mugs, and started splashing water at each other while singing '*Radhe Govinda*' in a tune made up by my brother. Our singing was interrupted only by our own laughter and the splashes of cool water from all directions. We had unbelievable fun that day. My mother, Perima and the other elders were resting and chatting while drinking filter coffee and munching on handmade murukkus in the kitchen area. The commotion from the courtyard made them wonder about what was going on there. Soon Amma walked in to check on us and was taken by complete surprise. All of us, soaked from head to toe and smiling from ear to ear, lined up before her and explained to her in excitement the wonderful game that we had discovered. I am not sure if she was very excited about it at the time, but I am certain that she would have been reminded of that incident whenever we played Holi in the later years with Gurudev.

Whether it was Papanasam or Bangalore, the games we were engaged in had a spiritual quality about them. We would sit cross-legged in front of a beautifully decorated Krishna idol with bowls of sweets neatly arranged in front of us. My brother would close his eyes and chant something with folded hands even as I would try imitating him while peeking constantly both at him and the sweets. Once I sneaked a small piece of sweet out of a bowl and stuffed it into my mouth. At the very next moment, my brother was looking at me with those big eyes and I had to quietly put the sweet back into the bowl from my mouth. I asked him, 'Why do we have to offer it to God if he doesn't really eat it?' 'He makes it sweeter and gives it back,' pat came the reply.

Chants and meditations were a regular part of our lives. Pitaji was a keen observer and would engage us in conversations and encourage us to think. Once, Pitaji shared with us an anecdote that had left a deep impression on his mind. He said, 'One fine morning, young Ravi was watching the other children play, and he said, "People are waiting for me, I must go to them" and he was just four. I knew the spirit within him was working as the small child uttered these words.'

It was around this time that Pitaji took us to Thangamma, a Sanskrit teacher who conducted daily Bhagavad Gita classes. She was reputed to have stayed with Mahatma Gandhi in his ashram. During the class, she began chanting '*Parthaaya prathibhoditam*' and waited for my brother to repeat. Little Ravi, instead, chose '*Bhagavata narayanena swayam*', completing the verse and astounding his teacher. She asked him verses from different chapters and he knew them all! The Sanskrit teacher declared to my father that his son was a prodigy.

Thangamma encouraged patriotic spirit in her students. In August, the month of India's independence, my brother and I would wake up at 6.00 a.m. and go on a prabhat pheri, a morning walk around the streets singing patriotic national songs such as '*Vande mataram*' and '*Jhanda uncha rahe humara*'.

Mahatma Gandhi had a significant influence on our family and childhood. My paternal grandfather stayed at Sabarmati Ashram and served Mahatma Gandhi for twenty years. Atthaiamma took her children to her parents' home and donated all ten and a half kilos of her gold jewellery to Gandhiji's ashram. She said to my grandfather, 'I will take care of the children. You go and serve the country.'

Pt Sudhakar Chaturvedi, a Vedic scholar who was a close associate of Mahatma Gandhi, was our neighbour in Bangalore. Born in 1897, he had taught the Bhagavad Gita to Gandhiji. The Mahatma used to call him Bangalori, since he hailed from Bangalore. When Kasturba was on her deathbed and Gandhiji realized that she may not survive the day, he had asked Pt Chaturvedi to read out the second chapter of the Gita. There is a verse in the Gita that describes the qualities of one who is established and centred in knowledge: Sthitapragna. Gandhiji said, 'Bangalori, today is a test for your Bapu. Let us see if I can maintain equanimity today. My wife and partner for over 50 years is leaving her body. I have imposed my will on her all the time, but she chose to stay with me until her last breath. She is a real saint.' He made this admission during Kasturba's last moments.

At another time, when the pundit was travelling by train with Gandhiji in Darjeeling, the train carriage separated and started rolling down the slope. At this juncture, when the lives of the train passengers were in grave danger, Gandhiji asked him to write a letter regarding the incident. Pt Chaturvedi, evidently flabbergasted, quipped, 'If we do not survive, no one will read it!' Gandhiji replied, 'And if we do survive, then this time would have been wasted if we did not write the letter.' He would share many such memorable anecdotes about the Mahatma, which my brother would, in turn, share with all of us.

During the partition of August 1947, Gandhiji was deeply pained. He was losing faith in all his close aides. When he came to know about the news of Hindus and Muslims slaughtering each other, he refused to believe it. To get a first-hand account, he sent Pt Chaturvedi to Lahore. Upon reaching the city, the pundit saw that it was the Hindus who were being tortured and killed in the area. He himself was attacked, stabbed several times, and buried neck deep in a sand pit but was thankfully saved by an army officer. When he narrated the situation to

Gandhiji, the Mahatma refused to believe him, saying that the pundit was prejudiced because he was a Hindu himself. Pt Chaturvedi was deeply hurt that Gandhiji had lost faith in him. Upset, he returned to Bangalore. Three days later, on 30 January 1948, Gandhiji was assassinated. The pundit would share this story with a note of regret about how he felt he had betrayed Gandhiji in his last days.

He had not formally taught anyone until my brother came along. He saw the interest little Ravi had in the Vedas and imparted him the knowledge he had. Until this time, doing puja was my brother's favourite pastime. This was the point when we started seeing in him a love for the Vedas and an inclination towards a formless, unmanifested divinity.

We had a small statue of Gandhiji in our home. One day, my brother asked Pitaji, 'Where is Gandhiji?' Pitaji said, 'He has become one with God.'

'If Gandhiji is with God, he deserves flowers like other gods, too, isn't it?'

My brother then put some flowers on the statue and wanted to place it among the other idols. 'You want to know why you should be there? Pitaji says you are one with the gods!', he said to Gandhiji's statue. The statue was rather heavy and he asked for my help to carry it. But Gandhiji's stick broke while we were trying to move it. We kept it down in front of the idols. With a smile, little Ravi said to Gandhiji, 'Your stick was weak anyway, but do not worry, I will give you a strong one.' When one of the elders eventually asked what Gandhiji's statue was doing in front of the gods, he replied, 'Anyone who has reached God is equivalent to God.'

3

PEARLS ON THE SHORES OF TIME

I HAVE ALWAYS loved the sea. It reminds me of infinity, endless vastness. Each wave, powerful, is part of the ocean yet distinct from it. When it rises, it is aware of itself as a wave, and as it recedes, it merges back with the ocean. Such is our life too. It has risen as this form yet it is very much a part of the divine.

As a young boy, my brother was deeply interested in our ancient culture. He would want to know the details of all the rituals and deities, and their significance. He would absorb all the explanations and later share them with me. His simple and direct narrations piqued my interest. I was curious by nature and asked hundreds of questions, looking for logical answers. Although I was not very easy to convince, when it came to my brother, I always accepted his arguments. We had a little lending library at home. We kept a ledger for the books and made entries when neighbourhood kids borrowed them. This way, Pitaji encouraged the children to read and know more about our country, its people, and its traditions.

Pitaji would narrate to us stories of saints and we would

later have fun enacting them. We would research more about the saints in our little library, and my brother would chalk out the characters and script the dialogues. We would then enact a play on the terrace of our Jayanagar house while the elders tried to take their afternoon nap below. My mother would complain, 'We sent you up to have some quiet in the house, but with the racket on the terrace, we couldn't sleep a wink! What were you all up to?'

The heat on the roof did not bother us one bit. We would use the towels that were hung for drying to fashion our costumes. My brother would dress up as Buddha and I and our friends from the neighbourhood would go around him chanting 'Buddham sharanam gacchami'. We would inevitably giggle so much that it was difficult even for the Buddha to contain his laughter! At other times, he would tie an orange towel around his head and hold a stick, imitating Adi Shankara. We would then follow him around chanting, 'Hara Hara Shankara, Jaya Jaya Shankara.' I would go to 'Shankara' seeking gyan—knowledge—and all I would get was a gentle tap on my head with the stick he was carrying. These little games were a lot of fun and we learnt so much about various saints. My brother would remember the birthdays of each of these saints and organize special events to celebrate the occasions. Even now this tradition continues as he celebrates someone or the other's birthday every day of the year! Besides saints, we would enact the lives of kings, queens, devis and devatas too. It gave us immense joy to wear the costumes that were painstakingly stitched for us by our aunt Vasantha. She used to enjoy dressing us up and would stand and admire her own creativity! Both my brother and I used to love playing our parts. We would continue to be in the skin of our characters long after the play was over and would eventually burst out laughing at our own acting. Once, when he was around eight years old, little Ravi choreographed a dance for a Kannada folk song. Ten of us performed the song at Thangamma teacher's house as part of the Gandhi Jayanti celebrations. '*Moodala manaya mutthina neerina erakkava hoida* ...', which means, when did the Lord put water inside a closed oyster shell and make it such a perfect round pearl! I never understood the meaning of all this at the time—I just had fun doing the steps—but my brother had an eye that noticed and glorified the small wonders around us. The Yoga Sutras say '*Vismayo yoga bhumika*', which means wonder is the preface of Yoga. Our days were wonderful then, and whenever I look back, I can't help but feel the wonder again.

We laughed while doing things that we liked. What's more, we laughed even when things were not to our liking—for instance, while drinking castor oil. This was our Sunday ritual. Pitaji, with a spoonful of the viscous liquid that was supposed to clean our stomach, would pretend to search for us. We would run around the house and finally hide under a cot. Pitaji would loudly ask everyone, 'Have you seen the children?' As usual, I would start giggling and Pitaji would find us. 'It is all because of your laughing,' my brother would chide me. 'I told you to be quiet!' The medicine would find its way down our throats encouraged by the deep but pleasant voice of Pitaji. Our father never forced anything on us. Everything was administered in a gentle and pleasant manner. Those were the special castor oil days!

But castor oil was not the only thing that we swallowed.

It was common for guests to arrive at our home anytime. As a result, Amma stored things like instant milk powder for emergency purposes, so that no one was caught wanting for such things. Although my brother and I loved the taste of milk powder, we were provided only fresh cow milk. So when Amma took a nap in the afternoons, we would search the kitchen specifically for the tin can in which the milk powder was stored. But she was one step ahead of us and would have already hidden it on one of the uppermost shelves where our hands could not reach! She knew our intentions, howsoever secretive we tried to be. We would talk to each other in sign language and giggle over our ingenious plans. Amma would act ignorant and let us indulge in our little secret game. But no sooner had we climbed up and found the tin can, Amma would arrive as if by magic. We would plead with her but to no avail. She would curtly dismiss us by saying, 'Not good for health'. But Atthaiamma would intervene, saying, 'Just give them one spoon. Nothing will happen!' Then Amma would not be able to refuse and a silent confrontation with the mother-in-law would ensue. Although Amma respected her, she did not want to lose the argument. In any case, we used to get what we wanted. Small instances could lead to minor frictions between a mother-in-law and her daughter-in-law. But my brother would tell Atthaiamma that Amma was all praise for her and tell Amma the same about Atthaiamma, thereby helping temper potential frictions between them.

I am reminded of those days as I look at this tin box of Nestle milk powder kept aside for my tea this morning in California. I sit and sip my cup of tea gazing at the ocean. Tastes and priorities change. Now I can have an entire box of milk powder anytime I want, but there is no urge for it. Life is so dynamic and ever changing like the waves. Still, some things remain unchanged.

My connection with the sea began with a holy dip at Rameshwaram. My father immersed me in the sea saying it was an auspicious day. I gasped for breath. But I knew I was safe in my father's arms, and with his eyes gazing at me with a reassuring smile that everything was going to be okay, I smiled back. I still remember that day. I must have been a baby, perhaps two-and-a-half years of age or so, and, of course, with my brother by my side. Pitaji immersed him in the sea too.

Rameshwaram, Kashi, Madurai Meenakshi—Pitaji took us to many grand and ancient temples even before we were four or five. The architecture and magnificence of these temples were awe-inspiring for us. While my brother would pray at the sanctum, I would observe the jewellery used for the decorations. On seeing the fully adorned Meenakshi, I reasoned that she could carry the weight of so much jewellery only because she was a goddess! My brother was very fond of the goddess in this form even at a time when he could barely speak. He would say 'Michini' in his attempt to say 'Meenakshi' while fondly holding a tiny idol of the goddess in his little palms. Similarly, 'Pillaiyar', the Tamil name for Ganesha, became 'Puraru.' Every year, during Ganesha Chaturthi, which falls between August and September, a clay idol of Ganesha was brought home for worship. Once the puja was completed, the idol was immersed in water. My brother, then about four years, took the small Ganesha idol decorated with flowers, place it in a basket, and kept it on his lap. He held on to it with great affection and did not want to part with it. He implored Amma to let him keep his 'Puraru'. Amma, while touched by the connection he felt with the idol, was also keen to keep the tradition. But it was not easy to explain why the ritual was necessary. She would try reasoning with little Ravi that 'Puraru' would come back next year if only he allowed him to go for now. Later on, Gurudev has explained that though the divine resides within us, the nature of our mind is such that it needs an external form to express its feelings. We assume the divine to be part of the idol and offer flowers, fruits, incense and prasad to it as an expression of our gratitude. Once the puja is over, we invite the divine back into our heart and immerse the idol. Certainly, our heart is a better place for the divine!

My brother had a collection of five or six idols of gods and goddesses at home. They were his favourite toys. The outer corridors of large temples in South India housed little shops that sold typical temple-related goodies—shloka books, incense, flowers, puja items and idols. When we went to the Kumbeshwara temple in Kumbakonam, little Ravi spotted a graceful brass statue of Nataraja which he wanted to take home. It was quite big and Amma and Pitaji were at a loss as to how to convince their seven-year-old son against taking it. Luckily, the young boy spotted a smaller version of the same deity, which we decided to buy. At home, all the idols would be brought out carefully and placed in individual bowls, decorated with sandal paste and flowers, and set afloat on the kitchen tank, which would always be full with water. The temples have a 'teppam' ceremony where the deities are decorated and taken for a boat ride across the temple pond. We had our own little 'teppam' in our pond at home in Papanasam and the whole family would enjoy this endearing ritual.

The days that I spent with my brother were precious. Ponds, lakes or seas are all made up of water, yet they are different. As we grow older, everything seems to remain the same, but the quality of the consciousness of the enjoyer undergoes a sea change. When we were small, we used to go to Marina beach in Chennai and eat a typical snack of '*thengaai maangaai pattaani chundal*'—cut raw mangoes mixed with coconut pieces and boiled peas—and immerse our feet in the sea waves. But the way I look at the sea has changed. I enjoy great calmness watching the waves now. So many waves—small, big, soft and rough—just like thoughts in the mind. Sometimes they come as tidal waves, and when they recede, it is like meditating, going back to the source. What a life the Master has given me! I marvel at my own good fortune. The Master is like this magnificent sea, seemingly calm, yet full of dynamism.

My brother, with a spark of mischief, once replaced the files in Pitaji's briefcase with toys. Although he kept on giggling after the incident, no one suspected anything mischievous. When Pitaji opened his briefcase in the conference room at his office, the toys fell out instead of his files! He came home in the evening with a big smile and shared with the family how little Ravi had lightened up the whole office atmosphere with his mischief. When I think of it, I am amazed at how Pitaji did not show any anger at all at that time and even encouraged our naughtiness.

One thing that I remember fondly about our bonding with Pitaji is his story telling. As a small child, my brother used to hop on to Pitaji's shoulder and say, 'Appa, tell me a story'. I would climb on to my father's other shoulder. Pitaji must have told us hundreds of stories. Gurudev always remembered them. Years later, on several occasions, when Pitaji travelled with him, Gurudev would ask him to share them again with us. Pitaji would tell a story from the scriptures and Gurudev would open our eyes to its deeper timeless meaning.

The stories were an easy way to change my mood. When jasmine flowers bloomed, my aunt, Vasantha attai, used to adorn my long braided hair with the flowers. I would wait for my father to come back from his work to shower me with his love. He would always praise me to the skies and make me feel important and happy. Sometimes, he would come home late from work and I would be asleep all bedecked with flowers. The next day I would keep a long face and he would instantly make me smile just by narrating stories of kings and queens. Dancing, play-acting, painting, making dolls, playing the veena, singing—we were immersed in so many activities that kept us busy through the day.

Vasantha attai was our first music teacher. She would make us sit in front of her and ask us to repeat a line after she had sung it. As she sang the notes 'Sa re ga ma pa da ni sa ...' we would gape at her mouth, wondering where the notes came from! My brother was curious more about the origin of sounds than the notes. Vasantha attai sometimes took him with her to musical concerts when he was just four or five, but he would often fall asleep on her lap just halfway through them. The same would happen when Pitaji took us to scriptural discourses of learned scholars who visited the city. We would be the only children at these gatherings. A few minutes into these talks and we would be fast asleep! Pitaji was of the view that awake or asleep, soaking in the vibration of such positive places was good for us. Today I see many children at satsangs, and it is fulfilling to see the new generation growing up in an environment of knowledge and meditation.

Beggars were a mystery to us. 'Why are they begging?', little Ravi once asked Amma. 'Because they are poor', Amma replied. 'But why are they poor?', my brother persisted. 'God made them poor', Pitaji intervened. Little Ravi said, 'I will ask God not to create beggars.' Pitaji would recollect this conversation often. 'What a mature resolve from a tender heart', he would say fondly.

My brother's caring attitude and sensitivity extended to all and sundry, be it to people, plants or animals. He easily befriended animals and loved dogs, cats, and even elephants, as is evident even now. If you observe him playing with Maheshwara, the resident elephant in the Bangalore ashram, it is amazing how they relate to each other! It is such a joy to watch Gurudev's expressions. When we were small, my father used to take us to big temples that had elephants. My brother wanted to touch those elephants, but I would shriek at just the thought of it! Even then my father made sure that I was blessed (touched!) by an elephant. He knew that otherwise I would pester him later. For whatever my brother did, I *had* to do. So much togetherness, but this was definitely not a competition! I never knew the definition or feeling of the word especially when it came to my brother. No such thing as sibling rivalry. We never heard or experienced the term.

One day, when my brother was about eight years old, he came from school and straightaway rushed to our store room. He was hiding something. Instantly my mother guessed that something was up—we could never hide anything from her! I was very excited and followed my brother to the store. She asked us what we were up to. He looked at her innocently trying to give nothing away. She was curious but also busy with her endless household chores, so she let the matter be for the time being. After a while, out came two small furry ears and shiny eyes, followed by a delicate 'meow'—a tiny kitten peeked out of my brother's school bag. Snuggled between the books it looked adorable. There was a momentary spark in my mother's eyes before she assumed a tough look. But that moment was enough for both of us and we somehow convinced her to keep the kitten at home. We fed it enthusiastically with an ink-filler, and we may have overfed it! We often checked on it to see if the kitten was sleeping or awake. Night came and as soon as the kitten was left alone, it started making a lot of noise! We had to wake up every now and then, which annoyed Amma. Of course, she needed some rest after having worked the whole day.

First thing the next morning, we went searching for its mother. Thankfully, she was nearby—perhaps all the meowing at night helped her find her kitten. But we missed the little kitten the whole day. I went around pretending to be the kitten, meowing away, while my brother laughed at my inability to act like one! At least I was happy that I was making him laugh. He was the one who always put a smile on my face. Well, that was our first kitten, but now in the ashram, we have many of them, especially the Shankari family. Five generations have resided here and they all look identical! Shankari always surfaced when Gurudev sat down for his lunch and made her presence felt with her meows. Gurudev would give her some curd rice, which she would happily eat and then vanish. She was never spotted when Gurudev was away touring. How strange is that!

As children, we used to create makeshift homes with matchboxes to take care of butterflies, caterpillars, frogs and worms. But the nosy being that I was, I would keep peeping in to check if they were still there, and in the process let them free! After a typical day of explorations, expeditions and games, we would still not rest and wait for Pitaji and his stories. He encouraged us to make our own stories. I once narrated the story of a beautiful queen who washed vessels. My brother made fun of me, 'How can a queen wash vessels?' We argued over this, and he won, of course, but I enjoyed losing to him. Later, Gurudev would make my story come true. Everyone who comes to the ashram participates in *seva* during advanced programs irrespective of their positions. For our joy to increase, we must share it with others. Giving is essential for spiritual growth. The willingness to share what we have and help others is called seva. Gurudev says that the best seva is helping someone understand the eternal nature of life.

One day, little Ravi learned that as people grew old, they die. As Atthaiamma was the eldest in the family, he thought she would die first. He was very close to her and this thought made him anxious. He shared a room with her and after everyone fell asleep, he used to wake up and watch her breathe. He would watch her belly go up and down and was happy as long as she snored loudly. Whenever she stopped snoring, he would wake her up. The hours would go by till he drifted off to sleep at around four in the morning. He dreamt that if she were to die, she would wake up on his touch. This continued for many months, and he would often fall asleep during the day. When Atthaiamma finally passed away, I was in my seventh grade and it happened during our exams. I remember that my brother did not touch her then for fear of her coming back to life.

There were many things that we learnt from Atthaiamma. If any of the provisions in the house got over, she said, for instance, 'The house is full of sugar and we have to buy some from the shop.' She never said something was empty or was not there. She believed there were angels around us who kept saying, 'tathastu', meaning, 'Let it be!' So she made sure that we only spoke positively. I sometimes came home from school in an irritable mood (more so because of hunger after having given away most of what my mother had packed for lunch). Atthaiamma would say, 'Go to that corner and leave your anger with the devatha (angel) there and come back.' In this way, we as children learned how to deal with our anger and negative emotions. This experience of freeing oneself from emotions is so much stronger now when we do the 'bowing down' in Art of Living programmes. Every direction has a presiding deity with several associated qualities. For example, anger belongs to the angel of the North. Recognizing that anger is not our nature; we can surrender our anger to the angel of the North and feel free.

Atthaiamma never discriminated between the poor and the well-off. For her there was no distinction between our own relatives and the relatives of our house help. She would receive them all like honoured guests and serve them bonda and kesari bhaath. No one who came home could leave without having something delicious to fill their stomach. She would say, 'Shivarudrappa's father has come, bring kesari bhaath for him', and my mother or Vasantha attai would quickly prepare the dishes. I never saw her complain. She was always smiling.

Atthaiamma was a strong lady with a great sense of humour. She was of a heavy build and, at times, lost her balance and fell. But she would simply laugh at herself and get back to her feet. This was amazing for me. How could someone fall and laugh about it? It takes great strength to laugh at oneself. But if one could do that, no one could take away one's smile. Pitaji used to say that while walking with our grandmother, holding her hand, little Ravi used to tell her, 'Grandma, you won't fall. I am holding your hand.' And he was all of three years at the time! Atthaiamma played an important role in our childhood. She used to light an oil lamp and wait for an hour every Friday between 6 and 7 p.m. in the doorway of our house for Goddess Lakshmi. This tradition continues even today with the Lakshmi puja that is performed on Fridays.

My maternal grandmother (Paati) had an orthodox approach to life. But when it came to my brother, she was open to his views and ready to accept changes that he suggested. There used to be the practice of untouchability those days. Some people, if not vegetarian, were not allowed inside our house. Swaminathan, the caretaker of our paddy fields, was one such person. My brother questioned this practice, saying that people's background made no real difference. When he was about seven, having convinced his grandmother, he went on a bicycle ride with Swaminathan, shocking the conservative neighbourhood.

In our Bangalore house, the daughter of our house help never went to school. Education for girls was not even considered necessary in many such families. But little Ravi questioned this. 'If Bhanu can go to school, why can't she go too?', he asked. I am not sure what explanations were given at that time, but the seeds of my passion to bring education to girl children were certainly sown then. Today, Gurudev has started over four hundred free schools in the most remote and rural areas in India to bring the gift of holistic education to underprivileged children. Over fifty-eight thousand children study in these schools and more than half of them are girls.

4

OCEAN IN A TEACUP

WE STARTED OUR education at a small Montessori school located inside the same compound as our house in Minerva circle. When my brother started school, I had to stay put at home as I was not old enough. This was not a very acceptable proposition for me and I started throwing tantrums. All the same, I would wait for him to return so we could continue with our entertainments. On the first day of his school, Atthaiamma had accompanied my brother. After dropping him off, she walked back home, only to realize that, unbeknownst to her, my brother had followed her home! Amma was quite amused. My brother's logic was that after Atthaiamma escorted him to school, she had to walk back alone. So he had to escort her back. 'What if she gets lost?' It was not that he was making up an excuse to skip school; he genuinely cared for his grandmother.

When we moved to Jayanagar, our school, Model Education Society, was in the same street as our house. It was about four hundred metres away and we would walk down to the school every day. The school building was simple with a thatched roof. Atthaiamma would walk with us holding our hands. There was barely any traffic those days. A few cyclists and an occasional car were all that we passed. Atthaiamma just loved having us around all the time. Every Monday, she would feel bad that we had to go to school. Any chocolates that came home while we were away were divided equally among all the seven members of the family—Pitaji, Amma, our grandmother, Uncle Subramaniam, Vasantha attai, my brother and me—and kept aside for us until we were back from school. When she distributed the chocolates, her share also was given to us.

My brother was popular among his friends and teachers alike. He was a soft-spoken child. The school recognized his extraordinary intelligence and gave him a double promotion from class one to three. However, he was never able to talk about things that interested other kids. Sports and movies did not matter much to him. He wondered why others did not seem to think about the meaning and purpose of life, the world, and the divine. 'I would see other children playing and fighting—I spent most of my time resolving their fights.'

Young Ravi could not play football. 'I would see a ball, look at my feet, and think, "I cannot kick anything away with these feet." My feet would not move.' Amma was concerned about my brother's lack of interest in sports. But he told her, 'I never really enjoy winning. I am not happy to see someone else lose either. If someone were to lose, I would not be happy. I am happy seeing others happy.'

At school, teachers and students came to my brother for advice and solace. They used to say, 'Somehow Ravi just dissolves our worries and problems. Being with him makes us feel light.' One of our teachers, Ms Shanti, sometimes even came home to meet my brother because she felt peace of mind in his presence. Many of my brother's friends, some from his class, some from higher classes, would walk back with us from school, just to give us company. Gurudev shared a very interesting anecdote related to one such walk. 'I was about seven or eight years old. While I was walking on the pavement with my friends, I tripped on a stone and fell. I fell unconscious for a few moments from the impact. During the time, I had a vision of a bluish cloud of energy that condensed into a soul. I saw Amma in a Devi temple in Kumbakonam circumambulating the temple tree. A pious and pure lady, I decided that she would be my mother. I then saw a grain of rice, the purest grain. It was like a mountain in front of me. I entered it. The grain was part of the prasad that Amma carried home from the temple. She offered it to Pitaji and I entered him through the grain. The soul stayed with the father for about three months before entering the mother.'

Amma used to worry that her young son was meditating or speaking philosophically most of the time. Pitaji was the one to reassure her that everything would be fine. When my brother was about seven years of age, his Upanayanam, the sacred thread ceremony, was performed. This is a ceremony during which the highest knowledge of the Brahman—the self—is whispered into the ears of a child. The Gayatri mantra is bestowed with the blessing of invoking brilliance and truth in the intellect of a child. When my brother performed Sandhyavandana, he took about an hour and a half, while our cousins took only ten minutes. Even as a child, he was deeply sincere about honouring sacred traditions. Today, thousands from every part of the world come to the ashram and learn to perform the Sandhyavandana. Gurudev explains, 'There are three states of consciousness—waking, dreaming and sleeping. At the junctures when one state ends and another state begins, something fantastic happens. You get a glimpse of that which is beyond the three. And that is the Divine. It is the basis of all creation. It removes all fears and gives a bigger dimension to life. This experience, transcending thought and emotions and going to another level of stillness, is called Sandhya. Vandana is adoring that inner state.'

People would advise Amma, 'Do not allow your son to do so much puja; he won't study properly'. So whenever he sat down to meditate, Amma would hurry him along. 'Not over yet? You're taking too long. Come on, hurry up! You have to study!' Years later, looking at Gurudev's busy tour schedule, Amma would say, 'You are always in Hari (hurry) ... and I am in Shiva!' Hari being the playful manifestation of divine energy and Shiva being stillness, the meditative aspect.

A few days after his thread ceremony, my brother went with his friends to learn swimming. A friend's father was going to teach them. They found a large village well to practice. These wells tended to be several hundred feet deep. Most of his friends already knew a little bit about swimming. He listened to the instructions from the parent, and in a moment of absolute fearlessness, jumped headlong into the water. First, it was moist air that gushed past his face and within moments he was several feet below the surface. No air, no light, just water all around and a feeling of plunging deeper and deeper into an abyss. All other sensations were fading when suddenly the sacred thread pressed hard against his skin and a force pulled his body upward. When he became conscious again, he was in the safety of our home. His friend's father had jumped in behind him, had barely managed to catch hold of his sacred thread, and pulled him out of the water. He was literally saved by a thread! My mother was beyond upset. Pitaji's face was grave but relieved. He said he had expected something ominous as he had seen a bad phase associated with water in my brother's horoscope. He had avoided going to any place with water bodies as far as he could but was happy that the phase was over now.

Time changes many things. A few years later, my brother was effortlessly swimming across the Ganga. He loves taking everyone along for a dip or on walks along the ancient river. He is in a very different space when he visits the Ganga. Standing on the banks and watching him, time seems to come to a standstill. Gurudev says often, 'When time freezes, you get a glimpse of eternity.'

'Anantha' is the one without an end, the eternal one. Ananthana Habba is celebrated in Karnataka, especially by the Madhva community, on the tenth day after Ganesh Chaturthi. After the puja on this day, a red thread with fourteen knots is tied on the hand. A devout Madhva lady, Sethu bai, lived just behind our house. On this particular day of puja, there were tasty puran polis that Sethu bai had made as prasad for devotees. Along with the sacred threads for the puja, she kept two extra puran polis for my brother and me. We jumped over the compound wall to reach her house in time for tying the thread and returned home proudly bearing the mark of Anantha (Lord Vishnu). While the threads were kept just for us, Sethu bai gave puran polis to the entire family. My mother, in turn, shared sweets with her.

Between the houses of Sethu bai's, Sarojamma's which was diagonally behind our house and the other neighbours who stayed close by, there would always be some exchange of food every day. Each one would make some new dish or the other and share with the others. In our house, my mother always prepared some extra food, 'This is for Sethu bai, this is for Sarojamma, and this is for '*pakkathu aathu mami*'—the next door aunty ...', she would say. Those were not small servings but full vessels as all members of each joint family had to have their share! Our next-door neighbours were especially fond of Amma's cooking and everyday some mouth-watering rasam would cross the compound wall from our kitchen to theirs. Sarojamma enjoyed having me and my brother around and often invited us home. She constantly wrote 'Sri Rama Jayam' in her notebook while she chatted with us or listened to music. It was almost an involuntary act.

Whenever people ask me about the difference between doing japa and invoking the guru mantra for meditation, I remember her. The mind very quickly learns to start processing anything repetitive even as it runs behind something new. The nature of the mind is to always keep running. But what happens to a mind that is established firmly in the present moment? If you do not recognize such a mind, you may end up saying, 'It's different!'

Although young Ravi was different from others, he was never out of place. He knew how to connect with people and was dear to everybody. Once, during a school programme, Gunakritha, a young girl, performed the dance of Devi Durga. Her charming oval face was clear and expressive. She had long, neat braided hair and wore a simple bright bindi as her only adornment. She did not use much make-up or other accessories but looked bright and beautiful. She was a good dancer. My brother was watching the performance intently, and at one particular moment, like a flash of lightning, he realized that he had a higher calling. 'In that fraction of a moment, I saw the face of each and every person in every country who was waiting for me ... the people who had come along with me to the planet. I knew I had family everywhere,' he later shared.

One of the boys in my class used to collect stamps and one day he brought a Mexican stamp to our class. It was very rare to see stamps from other countries in those days. Everybody was naturally curious about it. My brother told them, 'I can get more stamps for you. I have family there and am going there for vacations.' One vacation came, then another, but we never went anywhere except Papanasam. They stopped believing him. They wrote 'London', 'America' and 'Switzerland' on the doors of the toilet and teased him, 'See, he will go to London and come back'. 'They laughed because I didn't have any relatives abroad,' my brother would explain. He never saw malicious intentions behind anyone's actions. Still, he never used the school's restrooms because of this. My mother wondered why my brother spoke this way because she knew he never lied.

When I travelled abroad with Gurudev for the first time, the first person I met in each country that we visited would tell me, 'We have been waiting for him for so many years.' Each time this happened was a moment of revelation for me. I wondered with great joy, 'Who *is* he?' Gurudev says, 'I have never felt like a foreigner in any country. I feel at home everywhere and that I know everybody. I do not feel a difference between known, unknown, or new people. No one has ever been a stranger to me.'

I also used to collect stamps during our school days and Gurudev had promised to get me some when he would travel abroad. Several years later, when he went to Switzerland for the first time, he sent me a letter along with a packet of stamps, which I still have. He remembered a simple wish from years ago. He sent me letters with many stamps, sometimes more than what was needed for postage, so that I could add them to my collection.

Besides collecting stamps, I enjoyed reading books. Sometimes, I read without a break, even late into the evening. My mother used to think I was studying, but my brother would tell her, 'Amma, Bhanu is reading some novel instead of studying!' Of course, my mother did not want me to waste electricity on novels and I had to put the book away. I have rarely seen my brother reading books. But he could quote verses from ancient texts, and we wondered how he saw or read those books, let alone learn the difficult verses.

Pitaji often had learned guests visiting him at home. They sat and discussed scriptural knowledge. Pitaji encouraged us also to participate and listen. He organized talks, which he called 'Veda Bharathi', and invited everyone to attend. My brother and I also had to participate in these sessions. A few minutes into the talk and my brother's eyes would close gently and his head would lean forward. I would smile, fully convinced that he had gone to sleep. Until one learns to meditate, if one sees someone sitting with their eyes closed, the natural inference is that the person is sleeping. Who would have thought that a child would slip into deep meditation listening to higher scriptural knowledge? As we grew older, he would encourage questions on the deeper purpose of life and ask each of us to share our views. Young Ravi used to speak, quoting scriptures that I am sure he had never read, but it sounded so simple yet profound. I wondered how he knew so much. Trying to make sense of how he went through fourteen years of his schooling is like attempting to contain an ocean in a teacup.

Once, during an interview, the host asked Gurudev how he felt during his teenage years and he said, 'When I was twelve or thirteen, I used to feel that before coming into this body, I was everywhere, all pervading, and now I am here.'

As we grew up, I always wanted to be where my brother was, to the extent that our parents had to seek special permission for me to accompany him on class trips. I would be the only child from a junior class in a trip for the senior class. Like all siblings, at times we had our disagreements. Whenever I did something that displeased him, instead of yelling or fighting, he would sit calmly in a corner with his eyes closed. He would take to silence. I would go near him, make funny faces, and do everything to make him smile. Later, I learnt that only in silence could you find solutions, not in arguments.

There were three boys in our school who bullied and teased other students. My brother requested them to stop bullying students, but naturally they did not take kindly to this and waited until after class and chased him. My brother could understand their intentions. He took off, hid behind a tree, and ran home once the boys went past his hiding spot. He outsmarted them two days in a row, after which they became his friends and changed their ways. Gurudev often mentions that any emotion, be it negative or positive, lasts for a maximum of two days and a quarter.

Amma used to sing and was adept at playing the veena. She had mastered the fine art at a young age. My brother and I learned to play the veena from her. Sometimes, we caught him playing movie songs too! He even went on to win prizes for playing the instrument. Gurudev has jokingly said that he might have turned into a veena player had he not chosen the spiritual path. But for him even the veena has so much wisdom to offer. He says, 'The seven strings of the veena are like the seven layers of existence (the body, breath, mind, intellect, memory, ego and self). When they are in tune, in harmony, then life is mellifluous.'

Young Ravi attended high school at St. Joseph's college. One day, the principal called him and said that nobody from the college was participating in the inter-collegiate competition for Carnatic music. My brother replied, 'Why? I am there, I will do it.' He learnt to play a song on the veena and went on to win the first prize. The principal was very happy. When he came home with the winner's trophy, my mother was very surprised. The song that he played, 'Sudhamayi sudhanidhi', was set to the Carnatic raga Amritavarshini, meaning nectar shower. He won the prize with just two months of practice, but what was amazing was that when he played the raga, it would start drizzling!

My brother was deeply interested in poetry as well. He wrote a few poems in Kannada when he was about fourteen, which were published under the title Manjina Hanigalu, meaning dew drops. These poems were clear, deep and profound meditations on creation and the mysteries of life.

While we all knew that young Ravi was special, Subramaniam chittappa, my father's younger brother, looked upon young Ravi as his guru. Chittappa remained a bachelor, and if anyone were to ask him about it, he would say, 'I have two wonderful children—Ravi and Bhanu'. He recognized the divinity in young Ravi and considered him as his master. He said, 'Whenever I miss Gurudev, I hear him speaking to me, *enna chittappa?* (what is it, dear uncle?), a voice that will always remain with me.' He left his body in Gurudev's arms at the age of sixty. Chittappa had just returned from my cousin's wedding. Mohana and Shantha, two devotees from Mysore, were sitting in the living room of Manjula, singing songs. Gurudev and I were also there. Chittappa came out of the bathroom, walking slowly, holding on to the wall for support. Gurudev was meditating but suddenly opened his eyes and rushed towards him asking, 'enna chittappa?' He helped Chittappa to a bed. Chittappa sat on the bed beside Gurudev and leaned against him, holding his hands, and was no more. He was walking a few seconds before and in an instant his prana left him. I have never seen somebody relinquishing his life so easily. Gurudev later said Subramaniam chittappa was an avadhoot, the term referring to a realized soul who has transcended body consciousness and is not conditioned by social norms.

My brother completed his education with a Bachelor of Sciences degree. He says that he acquired the degree just to please his mother. He even went for job interviews, one memorably with a bank. He talked to the interviewers about meditation and the value of a calm mind. They offered him a job, but since my brother was not really interested, he chose to visit Rishikesh instead, on the banks of the Ganga, before returning to Bangalore.

I was studying philosophy in college. Lakshmi Tathacharya, though a Vishishtadvaiti, was our Advaita teacher. We had to learn about all three schools of Vedanta, and inter-college debates between students who represented various schools were a regular practice. Advaita sees oneness in creation. Vishistadvaita, on the other hand, sees a separation between the devotee and the divine and considers devotion as a path towards unity. Dvaita says that the creator and his creation are separate beings—an individual soul with its limited potential should find peace through the service of and devotion to the omnipotent. I was part of the Advaita group, but when I listened to the arguments of the other groups, I felt those were compelling, too. Although I did not have many counterarguments, in my heart of hearts, I felt there was something incomplete in the philosophies of the other schools. At home, I shared my apprehensions with my brother and asked him what the right way was. He just said 'Shivoham' ('I am Shiva, the supreme, undivided, infinite consciousness') and smiled. At that moment, my apprehensions vanished and a sea of calm enveloped my being.

One may have all the scriptural knowledge in the world, but only a master can translate it into an experience that leads one towards the truth. Gurudev often gives us the example of Hanuman, who talks of his relationship with Lord Rama. 'In the bodily form, I am your servant (Dvaita). As the Jiva (individual soul), I am part of you (Vishistadvaita) and as the Atma (the Self), there are no differences, we are one (Advaita).' The truth may seem contradictory but is actually multidimensional and not conflictual.

In his late teens, while he was still in college, an advertisement about transcendental meditation attracted my brother's attention. One day, he decided to visit the office of the organizers, where he met a lady who spoke to him pleasantly about meditation. He liked what she said and decided to attend the programme. When he was back, he initiated me, too, into meditation. He stayed in touch with the organizers, and they soon invited him to a teacher's training programme in Melkote. He attended, but on the way back, gave away everything he had in his suitcase, much to the dismay of our mother! After this training, he was called to Rishikesh, and after some advanced programmes that lasted several weeks, he returned home.

It was around this time that a marriage proposal had come for me. I was still in college. My mother and aunts felt that I was still too young, but Pitaji felt that the wedding will do me good. 'He is a spiritual person and will be good for her,' he said. My cousins and relatives were quite excited about the marriage, and everybody was involved. Being a close-knit family, my aunts and uncles had their own views about what to do and how to go about things, be it about clothes, invitations, jewellery or food. Most of the family members in Papanasam were busy with the preparations. Chakklis, the quintessential South Indian spiral-shaped snack, were prepared in different sizes—the closer the relative, the bigger the size of the chakkli that was on offer. Laddoos, mysore paks, chow-chows—small packets of several yummy delicacies—were packed along with the traditional tamboolam, consisting of betel leaves, betel nuts and a coconut, as gift for the guests.

I was excited about the new saris and jewellery—it was a busy and happy time before the wedding. The entire family from Papanasam attended the wedding, which took place in Bangalore, and it was a grand affair. After marriage, I stayed back at Manjula to complete my studies.

One day, my brother started suffering from a terrible headache, which left the whole family anxious. The pain was unbearable and no medicine was effective in alleviating it. I was in tears, and Pitaji and Amma tried everything in their power but to no avail. The pain lasted for a good few hours before subsiding on its own. We never knew why it came or how it went but we were grateful, nevertheless, that it was over. When I think back about it, I wonder if the headache was a result of physiological changes that happened in succession as channels of energy gradually opened up in him—similar to a bud blooming to become a flower. A couple of weeks later, he was once again invited to Rishikesh as Maharishi Mahesh Yogi, the Seer and creator of the transcendental meditation technique, had arrived there. The excitement at the prospect of meeting him was palpable. We knew this meeting was important for young Ravi but were unprepared for what was to happen. Our lives were about to change completely.

5

A CLOSE BOND

THE FRAGRANCE OF a moment is spread by words that flow out of a serene mind. Memories rise one after another in this tranquil moment of gazing into the sea, which is welling up with waves of joy and beauty. When one has a guru, one's whole existence takes a sublime form. Every breeze feels like a gentle caress, the sunshine brightens one up, and the moonlight beckons one into a dream.

Young Ravi was at an age when most young people would dream of a good job and a great salary. But his world was far removed from all of these aspirations. My brother met Maharishi in Rishikesh, and when he came back home, he stayed only for a few days, just to do some paperwork. He was going to accompany Maharishi to Switzerland as a student of the Maharishi European Research University (MERU). He was away for close to two years.

This was a very long time for all of us, and letters and a few phone calls were our only solace. When his letters came, Amma would read them first while I waited for my turn, and between us we shared tears of joy and longing on reading his words. One of the letters said, 'All colours are beautiful, and it is difficult to choose between them. So I decided to wear white, which includes all colours.' Another letter spoke of how barbers were few in Switzerland and haircuts, expensive. Finally, a letter with news of his date of return arrived. International flights did not land in Bangalore those days and my brother had to go to Chennai and take a connecting flight to Bangalore. Pitaji and I went to the airport to receive him. Our ears were tuned to arrival announcements and eyes glued to exit doors from which passengers emerged in bursts every few minutes.

My brother had left for Switzerland attired in simple trousers and a shirt. I expected him to look the same when he returned. When he arrived, our eyes met, and the love and depth in those eyes were unmistakable. Although I wanted to believe that the person before me was my brother, many things had changed. In flowing white robes and long hair, he looked ethereal, and the appearance looked perfectly natural to him. His hair touched his shoulders, and it looked luxurious. His voice was soft and gentle, seemingly slower than before, yet it carried an unmistakable energy. My heart was in conflict, struggling to believe that my brother was still the same, but my mind was stunned into acceptance that he had changed. Pitaji took charge of his luggage and we started our drive back home.

'What is this avatar of yours?', the words came pouring out of Amma the instant she saw her son. He smiled as their eyes met, the only answer to her question. She studied him carefully, absorbing every detail. The subtle strength of his glowing presence was unmistakable, and the aura had a palpable quality about it. He was always considered handsome, and our aunts and uncles would complement him and tell my mother that he was the 'Kamal Haasan' (a popular film actor) of our house. But the charm and beauty that he exuded now was incomparable and different. While we were experiencing these changes, I could see that a battle was raging in my mother's head between 'he has changed' and 'he is my son.'

My mother used to serve him food with much love, but now she also experienced a special reverence for him. We were not prepared for the changes in his attire and had to replace all his trousers and shirts. I went shopping in Jayanagar to get some dhotis and kurtas. We tried our best to act normal but knew it was just pretence. Who was going to bell the cat? And even if we wanted to, how would we go about the task? Somehow, I could not argue with him anymore. When words flowed out of him in that familiar, gentle tone, they were final and had a subtle authority to them. The voice was not coming out of the limitations of a corporeal body but was connected to a field that was beyond and unknown to us. Time and again, I would look into his eyes, which were ever so reassuring, and comfort myself that he was still with me.

The days passed by quickly and it was time for him to leave again. His travels were frequent and he was away several months at a stretch. He came home for short visits, which were made even shorter by Maharishi's phone calls. I have heard his deep, resonating voice on the phone. Maharishi would say 'Ravi ...' and, lo and behold, there would be a change in my brother's schedule. Perhaps Maharishi knew how loving our family was and perhaps because of this he never let my brother stay at home for too long.

In Gurudev was a beautiful blend of the Vedas and science,

thanks to his association with Maharishi, whose techniques of transcendental meditation were popular across the world. When asked about their first meeting, my brother simply said, 'I recognized him and he recognized me.' Maharishi was conducting conferences across India to bring scientists and Vedic scholars together on a single platform. My brother was a science student and enjoyed studying physics. He entertained other students with his wit and humour and was missed when he was away from his classes for long. However, he was invited to speak in the same class later.

He used to come home for a few days between the conferences, during which time he would be engrossed with his practices behind the closed doors of a small study upstairs. Curious, I would peep through the keyhole to see what he was up to. One such time, I was taken aback when I found him levitating off the floor! I was amazed and excited at the prospect of learning this from him. Later I came to know that there were many others along with him who were practising these techniques and I wanted him to teach me too. But when I asked him about it, all I got were smiles. That little room has been host to many spiritual people, healers, astrologers, among other learned people, whom Gurudev used to invite at different times. They would all give us the same message, 'You have no idea who he is and you will see how the whole world will come to him. You are very fortunate that he is with you.'

My husband, whom I call Anna, was working in Pondicherry at the time. Visiting the city was like a holiday for me. I would indulge in shopping, buying handbags and shoes, and come back and share the things I got from my husband with my friends—those were my 'girly' days. Once I finished college, I moved to Pondicherry to live with him. My husband once organized a talk for my brother at Jipmer, a renowned medical school based in Pondicherry. My brother spoke about meditation for doctors, and at the interactive session, the doctors asked specific questions about human physiology and were surprised at his deep knowledge of surgery and medicine. Here was someone who could talk about spiritual practices and their impact on the human body! They soon invited him to a second visit and requested him to inaugurate and speak at a key seminar.

After this event, we decided to drive to the Shaneeshwara temple in Thirunallar, Tamil Nadu. While we were on our way, at around seven in the morning, my brother asked Anna if he could get a piece of yellow cloth and a hundred rupees in one-rupee coins. While Anna wondered where to get the coins at such an early hour in a small town, my brother started giving clear instructions to the driver as if he was well-versed with the route although this was the first time we were visiting the area! He asked the driver to stop outside a tiny shop and instructed Anna to check with the shop's owner. A little hesitantly, my husband asked the shop owner if he would have a yellow cloth—and he did. Anna then asked for the coins too. The shop owner offered to check and started counting the coins in his box. To our surprise, when he finished counting, he had the exact change! When Gurudev gives one a task, he not only shows the way but offers guidance at every step. When one follows his instructions, one is amazed at what unfolds.

Mission accomplished, Anna came back to the car, and we proceeded towards the temple. But my brother, as usual, had other ideas and was out on his own for a while before joining us. Once again, he gave instructions to the driver and we reached a simple house where he told us to have darshan of the man who lived there. He was dark complexioned with one of his eyes only partially open. His physique was somewhat misshapen and contorted as well—we bowed down to him and came out of his house. My brother said that our visit was complete now, but Anna told him that a puja had been organized at the temple and that people were waiting for us. So, we proceeded to the temple together. About six months later, Anna had to visit the same area in relation to his work. He drove through the same route and could neither find the house nor the old man there.

A few months after this, I was pregnant with my first child and was at my parents' house in Bangalore. Although my brother was always busy travelling and giving talks, he managed to be at home for every important occasion. He was there for the seemantham (baby shower) and at the time of the child's birth too. He held the baby in his arms and gently rocked it to sleep. He stayed until the naming ceremony but was soon travelling and giving talks again.

My brother toured several cities, often in various countries, to talk about the importance of meditation. When he returned, he invariably gave away whatever he had. But once, after returning from an international tour, he kept one particular shawl with himself. It had a small mango-shaped motif embroidered on its corners in brown silk thread. He told us that many people had liked the shawl so much that if he had given it away to one person, the others would have felt bad!

Young Ravi accompanied Maharishi to Switzerland several times. We were eager to hear about his experiences, have a glimpse of his days there, and re-live them through his words. We had a swing in our porch with a wooden tile-inlaid bench arranged perpendicular to it. This made for a comfortable seating arrangement for chatting and getting some fresh air, especially in the evenings. All of us would sit around him, ears attuned only to the sound of his voice. He shared an interesting anecdote one day. 'A few of us were sitting with Maharishi, who was being briefed about some problems related to the transcendental meditation movement in America. Maharishi said, "Once you are at the top, the peak, there is no plateau. So whoever reaches the peak must come down." And I quipped, "There is no competition for depth." At this, Maharishi chuckled with a twinkle in his eye.'

My brother says that he has never met anyone with as profound a mind as Maharishi's. Perhaps that is the reason why everyone—young and old, scientists and simple people—could relate to him. He told us that when Maharishi met Baba Muktananda, the founder of Siddha Yoga, or Anandamayi Ma, the famous spiritual leader from Bengal, people expected intense philosophical exchanges between them. However, to peoples' amazement, they would just exchange pleasantries—those were more of joyful occasions of getting together than opportunities for discussing the complexities of atma or paramatma.

In such moments, when memories of my brother's days with Maharishi came alive, we caught glimpses of their exchange, which sometimes appeared deep and at other times indiscernible. He shared another incident, which took place at a gathering of six to seven pundits who had come to meet Maharishi in the late 1970s in Delhi.

A Sanatani pundit was chanting a Sanskrit verse in praise of Saraswati, the goddess of learning. The verse described Saraswati as 'Goddess clad in white, exuding the essence of Brahman in thought and expression. The Original One, spread all over the world, holding a rosary and the scriptures.' An Arya Samaj pundit was trying to refute the import of the verse. What ensued was a heated argument. Maharishi was sitting there, enjoying the whole argument. He glanced at me, playing with his mala and gesturing towards himself. He repeated the gestures to make sure that I understood what he was hinting at. Maharishi sat smiling, clad in white, exuding the essence of Brahman in thought and expression. The Original One, spread all over the world, holding a mala, with a book before him! He went on to explain that Saraswati is that consciousness in which total knowledge is manifested: The One without a second. The pundits who were busy arguing missed the subtlety of his gestures. Often people make affirmations such as 'I am Brahman, the self' in the name of self-awareness or spiritual realization. Maharishi was against any such affirmation as these were possible only at the level of thought, at a gross level, and not at the realm of experience.

While on the one hand we talked about Saraswati with a rosary and scriptures, which meant the refinement of intellect, on the other, we also considered a Saraswati who played the veena, which meant the refinement of feelings. My mother played the veena very well and so did my brother and I. Whenever he came home, we took out time to play the veena together. Hindolam, Sree, Shanmughapriya, Shivaranjani and Revathi—various ragas flowed one after the other, and the notes, arising in perfect harmony, filled my senses. The mind ceased to exist, and in that space, the being simply floated along with the melody.

Music was not a part of Maharishi's movement. But my brother, being a connoisseur of art, shared an anecdote related to Kalki Gardens, home to renowned musician M.S. Subbulakshmi and her husband T. Sadashivam. This facility was being purchased by Maharishi's organization, and before the keys were handed over, my brother conducted a puja there. M.S. sang at the puja and shared that she could experience the presence of the Divine Mother that day.

Kalki Gardens, like other such facilities, was used to train young boys to become priests. One of those pundits was at the ashram recently to conduct a wedding. He was standing with hundreds of others as Gurudev was driving past on his buggy after a satsang. Gurudev later met the pundit at his kutir. They were meeting after almost three decades. He chanted a few verses from the Samaveda and after the recitation shared that he was one of the students trained at Kalki Gardens. 'My Veda books were torn and you had pasted them back together for me. I was ten at the time,' he recalled. Gurudev smiled and enquired about his teachers and the school. He had not really 'known' that this pundit had come from Kalki, yet he knew, which was not a matter of memory, but a matter of being connected with the entire creation. Someone had once asked Gurudev, 'When a person needs you, how do you know it?' 'You are like the hair on my head' he replied. At the time he had such a lot of hair that it would take about half an hour just to comb it. 'I do not really know how many strands there are but even if one is pulled a little, I know exactly where it is.'

My brother was given the charge of spreading Vedic

wisdom, so he travelled across cities to reach out to the local youth through various programmes. Vishnu Bhatt was a trainee in one such programme. Once, along with Vishnu, my brother set off for Amarnath. The journey to the holy place was dangerous. If one were not careful, one could slip and fall from the narrow icy paths that led to the cave. My brother was riding a mule, supposedly trained for this arduous journey. However, the mule seemed to have a mind of its own and was walking recklessly along the outer edges of the path instead of staying close to the mountain. Somehow the duo managed to reach the shrine, did darshan of the Shiva lingam, and returned safely. It was such a relief to get off the mule! Vishnu later told me that they had met a nadi reader (a reader of palm leaves) after the temple visit, who had told him, 'Even animals feel deeply connected to Gurudev. The mule that he rode was thinking, "Today the divine has chosen me as his vehicle, so why should I worry?" That was the reason for the mule's confident stride.'

Once, another palm-leaf reader came searching for our house, claiming that his leaf had predicted that there was a young saint there who was verily the manifestation of the Divine Mother herself. He also said that if one were to offer a lotus to my brother on Fridays, one's wishes would be fulfilled. He came home carrying a garland of 108 lotuses, which he offered to my brother. It was amazing for us to hear it at that time—that we lived with one who could fulfil wishes. However, we did know that my brother managed to fulfil even the most unreasonable tasks that Maharishi had set for him. These tasks were an opportunity to step beyond reason and open up to higher possibilities. My brother spoke of those days laughingly, but these stories would inspire us to break the narrow boundaries that we'd set for ourselves. He said, 'Maharishi once planned a programme for ten thousand people in his Faridabad ashram and we arranged boarding and lodging for that number. We advertised the programme in newspapers, and a lot of effort went into setting it up. But on the big day, only ten people turned up. When I mentioned this to Maharishi, he chuckled and said, "Each of them is worth a thousand people." The next time, we planned for twenty thousand people. "I never look back, I simply keep moving forward," Maharishi used to say.'

In 1980 Maharishi wanted my brother to organize a yagna along with a Vedic conference in Noida. The event was such as success that Maharishi made plans for an even bigger yagna around the festival of Diwali to be performed by 6000 pundits. A few weeks before the event, young Ravi had to travel with him to Switzerland, and preparations for the ritual were left to others in the organization. For the ceremony, Maharishi wanted everything to be in yellow as far as the eye could see as the colour was associated with Goddess Lakshmi. So all the sweets and decorations were yellow in colour; gold coins from different countries were made available for the event. But when my brother returned from Switzerland with 3000 international guests who were to witness the yagna, he realized that there were serious lapses in arrangements. In fact, many of the pundits who were recruited were not good enough for the job. But it was too late.

Maharishi asked young Ravi to look into the reasons behind the lapses and ensuing chaos. My brother quickly realized that kickbacks had been received for the recruitment of the so-called pundits. But since many of them were from the state of Bihar, a rumour was spread that my brother disliked Biharis. Several people cautioned him against going to Noida as they anticipated trouble, but he still decided to go ahead. He was confronted by over a thousand Biharis who were brandishing black flags and burning torches, shouting slogans against him and threatening to set his car on fire. My brother, however, was unfazed and told the mob that they could proceed to do whatever they wanted provided he was allowed to speak for half an hour. Having secured a reprieve, he reasoned that he had nothing against Biharis, but if yagnas were not performed properly, it could cause harm not only to the country but also to the people who performed them. He added that the pundits should take a test, and those who could not qualify could be given other jobs. The negotiations proved to be fruitful, and he managed to settle the matter amicably.

Similarly, once, just a day before Akshaya Tritiya (third day after the new moon in May), Maharishi summoned several Vedic pundits and asked them to perform bhoomi puja to establish new Vedic centres across India. Though the organization had no land in any of these areas, he insisted that bhoomi puja be done immediately and would not take 'no' for an answer. Although such tasks seem mind-boggling and rather impractical, it helps the spiritually oriented to move beyond doership. Maharishi wanted people to act at once and his deadline would be the day before! Young Ravi somehow managed to identify suitable plots and arranged the pujas. In yet another instance, Maharishi wanted 600 pundits from Kashi to be brought for a special puja. The pundits of Kashi never leave their city and, as a result, everyone thought the task was impossible as the ritual was planned keeping not just one or two pundits in mind but 600 of them. Young Ravi, however, brought all of them together for the ritual at the appointed hour.

My brother's challenges increased as the days passed by. There were many who could not understand or accept why Maharishi treated him with so much love and honour. Several leaders, officials and spiritual leaders had grown very fond of him and came seeking his company and blessings. Probably because of this, some in the organization wanted him to be put in charge of a Vedic school in Noida, far from the public eye. There were instances when his phone lines were cut off, car tyres punctured on a day when he was expecting dignitaries for a banquet, or his cook dismissed on some minor pretext. Still, young Ravi managed to pull off the responsibilities delegated to him. He once said, 'One day, during such a challenging situation, awake at night and looking out of the window, I saw the watchman of the building monitoring the movement of vehicles. I watched him for a while. He was simply a witness to the flow of people, responsible for their movement. Yet he was a witness. Similarly, we are also witnesses to our responsibilities.' This was how he explained his ability to manage everything smoothly despite the various obstacles. Although my brother never complained, Maharishi found out about his troubles and asked him why he never reported them to him. My brother said, 'You have so much to attend to. I want to lessen your burden, not add to it.' Even at home, he never complained about anything. He would narrate things to us as if it was another interesting story.

During his days with Maharishi, my brother had the

opportunity to meet many spiritual leaders. Not far from Maharishi's ashram in Noida, in a village called Kotla, lived a saint known as Goliwale Baba. Baba had been an officer in the Indian cavalry when he was shot at in a war. The bullet that pierced him created such an impact on his nervous system that it resulted in his enlightenment. People in the village sought his help for their problems. Although he was keen on imparting spiritual knowledge, all they wanted was material help. Young Ravi often visited Goliwale Baba, who was very fond of him. While speaking of the Baba, he said, 'I had just one aversion at that time—flies—and when I visited the Baba, I was covered from head to toe with flies. I wasn't used to it and was uncomfortable. He saw this and told me, "Just let them be", and with those words the last aversion left me.'

Lakshman Joo, of the Kashmiri Shaivism tradition, was another holy person who had met young Ravi. He shared his concern with him on the state of Kashmir, his wish to bring peace there, and about continuing the tradition of Kashmiri Shaivism. Gurudev, during a recent conference on Kashmiri Shaivism in the Bangalore ashram, mentioned that Lakshman Joo's soul must certainly have found peace seeing the progress made on both his wishes.

Young Ravi had spent some time with Maharishi at the Gita Bhavan in Rishikesh. When Maharishi organized a congregation of spiritual people, my brother was entrusted with the task of welcoming them and taking care of their needs. Although my brother was young at that time, Maharishi recognized his abilities and sent him to various places in India and abroad to give talks on science and the Vedas. It was around this time that he decided to grow a beard. 'To look a little mature,' he would explain later, 'as the people I had to teach meditation did not take me seriously because of my age.' Scholars and intellectuals would ask my brother about the learned teacher of meditation, and my brother would have to tell them, a little embarrassedly, 'It is me who you are looking for!'

Pitaji was very supportive of my brother and accompanied him wherever possible. He once shared his observation on his son, 'He is innocent like a child and learned like a scholar. This scholarly innocence appeals to everybody. His laughter, singing, meditation, all blended into one, is not common in saints.' Although Pitaji was probably the one who was most prepared for the changes that we were witnessing, he, too, missed his son and would often tell others, 'Slowly, as he grew up, I found that he had to be away from home more and more. He was travelling at least ten out of twelve months. But the distance and time did not change our relationship. Where there is love, space and time disappears. Whenever he came, he ate with us, joked with us, and the family atmosphere was intimate. I have always felt him to be an exceptionally affectionate son. Although he is now a world-famous guru, he is still my loving child and master.'

When Maharishi brought a shy young Ravi to Anandamayi Ma, she said, 'Ah, you have brought me the Ganga.' My brother wondered what she was talking about. Anandamayi Ma continued, 'You have brought me the one who will wash away the ignorance of the world.' Maharishi was very proud of young Ravi and used to say, 'The sun (Ravi) rises and there will be light everywhere'.

6

THE PROPHECY

YEARS PASSED BY as young Ravi ceaselessly travelled across the globe with Maharishi. But his visions of people who were waiting for him continued. These visions appeared and passed like clouds in the blue sky, but with time, the passing clouds were turning into regular reminders, acting as a gentle pull towards an unknown path whose call was growing intense. Perhaps the time had come for a new beginning.

But before taking any decision, my brother decided to meet Devraha Baba, an old saint who lived on the banks of the Ganga. He arrived at dusk, and the boatman was initially reluctant to take him as he thought it was getting too dark and the Baba would not see anyone so late. Nevertheless, when my brother insisted, the boatman agreed. The silence in the air was interrupted only by the sound of the rowing. The boat moved ahead at a steady pace across the majestic river.

As soon as it arrived, the old saint came out and greeted young Ravi, 'Oh my son, you have come!' Usually, the Baba gave sweets to his visitors, but he gave a watermelon to my brother and said, 'Water has to flow. If it stops, it would stagnate. Satsang should also flow as it spreads grace across the world. Bring Satsang everywhere in the world'. The boatman exclaimed that he had never witnessed anything like that in his life. The saint was waiting for him, which was quite unusual. Giving a watermelon was unexpected as well. The message was loud and clear. Young Ravi had to start on his own and spread his wisdom through the world. But the toughest decision was leaving Maharishi.

In the late 1970s, Maharishi wanted to open a Vedic school in Bangalore for which Pitaji had recruited 175 students. However, the organization soon decided to consolidate all the schools and relocate the children to a place near Delhi. As they were all from the southern part of India, it was difficult for the children to adapt to the new environment. So they wanted to come back. But their education had to continue. So my brother decided to take over the school, though everyone around him was baffled at the decision. This was clearly the first time that he was taking up an initiative on his own. He chose to stand by the needs of the children despite the friction it caused between him and the organization.

One night, young Ravi was at the Hubli railway station with tickets to two different destinations. One train would leave for Bangalore where a few people from Maharishi's movement were waiting to take him to Delhi for a talk. The other train would take him to Solapur. On the one hand was an established organization with all the infrastructure and facilities and, on the other, was the vision he had for the people. He later said, 'I knew that if I took the train to Solapur, something new would begin. People were waiting for me all over the world and, therefore, I decided to take the train to Solapur.' This resulted in the birth of the Art of Living movement.

The school was the first project that my brother undertook once he left Maharishi's movement. For six months, the children stayed at our home—eating, sleeping, bathing and learning. It was Diwali time, and I remember how the kids, all 175 of them, waited in line to have oil massaged on their little heads by my father who sat with a cup of warm oil and a determined face—it looked as if he was on a mission. They all bathed in groups at a small well behind our house before getting ready for Diwali. One of those days, a gentleman approached my brother with the keys to his house, which was called Gurukripa. He was moving to New York and he offered his large house for the children. Similarly, another gentleman offered rice and pulses. 'I never asked for anything. Whatever was needed would come,' said Gurudev. This was the beginning of the Ved Vignan Maha Vidya Peeth, where hundreds of children continue to be trained in the Vedic tradition even to this today. The school is now located within the Bangalore ashram campus.

Gurudev's travels continued within India, meeting holy people, teaching meditation, giving talks, and interacting with the people who were waiting for him. His hair had by now grown longer and he sported a small beard. On one occasion, he was returning from Mysore by train. In the carriage, there was a Muslim gentleman who seemed to be in distress. He started conversing with my brother and requested for his advice. Nearly twenty years later, as we were taking a walk in the Vrindavan Gardens, Mysore, this man would come running over with his whole family and fall at my brother's feet. He was delighted to see Gurudev again and shared that his whole life had transformed after their meeting. All these years he was hoping to catch a glimpse of him, and although the meeting took place after two decades, the recognition was instantaneous.

Those who could 'recognize' my brother included holy people and astrologers, among others—people who had a deeper connection with the world could predict that an unstoppable wave of spirituality was rising within my brother, which would sweep the whole world off its feet and soak it with his wisdom. Among the several predictions, one was especially remarkable. Young Ravi was on a train journey from Delhi to Varanasi and was standing by the open door of his carriage with the wind blowing into his hair, gazing at the countryside that was flashing past. The ticket examiner approached him and started conversing with him and told him that he had had a powerful vision.

'Where is this world moving to? People are running crazily behind money ... What we see is nothing. The real world is different. If one comes from the real world, this world would look very dry.' Perhaps he thought that the young guru would understand what he had experienced. My brother asked the man, 'What do you see?' The man replied, 'I see that the supreme Lord has sent a person to this world. I see a sun with two swans on his either side. Wherever he goes, there will be an awakening, and he will bring solace to the minds of people. God is not going to come wearing a crown; he would take the form of a saint. And only the lucky ones would be able to meet him.'

7

THE COSMIC RHYTHM

MEDITATION IS LIKE smiling to oneself, but to be able to see that smile, the mirror has to be clean. Having taught the art of meditation to people across the world, Gurudev (this is how people began to address him by now and I caught on very quickly!) felt the need for a technique that would make meditation easier for people. It was the time of Navaratri, and he decided to observe silence for a period of ten days.

One of our neighbours, Mr Ashok, had a farmhouse near Kengeri, a few kilometres away from our place, which he offered for my brother's stay during the time. The farmhouse was full of coconut trees. As we drove in, we saw a pair of trees fused at the base. They parted somewhere in the middle and arched outwards. It was a picturesque sight. The house was unoccupied and tucked away in a pocket of serenity. Gurudev stayed there for twenty-one days and observed silence during the last ten. Silence could be practised at the level of word, thought or action, and I was witness to all three during those ten days. Once Gurudev went into observance, he did not venture out even to eat. The food, including fruits, remained untouched. Even the small pot of drinking water remained as it was. We routinely visited him, but there would hardly be any communication. Although at times we could not even meet him, we could feel his silent presence.

Conversing with Gurudev is special, but being in his presence has an inexpressible depth. My brother often says, 'Silence is soul to soul communication.' After the ten-day observance, an inspiring spark for a new technique had been kindled in him. The process was set in motion and with time it would refine itself.

A few months later, in March 1982, he travelled to the banks of River Bhadravati, near Shimoga in Karnataka. The river's crystal clear water flowed joyfully as the sky revealed its boundless expanse of unblemished blue. Lush green hillocks dotted the horizon and the pleasant air gave in to the gentle demands of the river current. There were no sounds except for nature's murmurs. My brother sat facing the river, and at an auspicious moment a delicate rhythm that accompanied the chant of 'So Ham' flowed through him—at first slow, then quicker, and then even more quickly. A cosmic rhythm that would enable perfect harmony had come into being. Gurudev called it Sudarshan Kriya—'Su' meaning proper and 'Darshan' meaning vision. Literally, it meant an action that enables proper vision, but in reality it was about whispering infinity into the ears of each of the people who came to him.

When asked about the Kriya, he said, 'I had been travelling the world teaching yoga and meditation. Still, I had been concerned about helping people lead a happy life. There was something amiss. Though people followed the practices that I taught them, their lives were still locked in compartments, and their outer behaviour differed from their inner being. I kept thinking of ways to bridge the gap between this inner silence and their outer expressions of life. Sudarshan Kriya came as an inspired solution. Nature knows what to give and when to give it. I started teaching this Kriya and people started experiencing great things.'

Gurudev was quick to impart this new-found knowledge to a few people in Shimoga itself. When he returned to Bangalore, we organized a two-day course for him to teach this new Kriya at the Ma Anandamayi hall in Jayanagar. I, along with Amma and Pitaji, participated in the programme, which was called 'Come and meet yourself!' Pitaji, very enthusiastic, invited his friends and acquaintances from the Rotary Club to attend the course.

The programme would start in the morning and finish only late into the night at about 10.30 p.m. with hardly any breaks. It was not easy for many to cope with its intensity, and some left just after the first day. But those who stayed back experienced phenomenal transformation and gained access to a deeper knowledge that was beginning to blossom from within them. I experienced Sudarshan Kriya for the first time during the programme. With every breath that I took along with the rhythmic chant of 'So Ham', a gentle wave of peace arose in me and receded into the vastness of an ocean. After a point, only the subtle movement of breath remained, and the entire existence felt as if it was compressed and contained in that single moment. While relaxing after the Kriya, my consciousness expanded to a space beyond the room, encompassing the whole planet and the sky. I was everywhere and nowhere. I experienced energy associated with Krishna, and my mother experienced Jesus Christ. Coming from an orthodox Hindu family, she did not know much about Christ, yet she experienced the love and compassion in him. We completed the course with exceptionally high energy levels. My second son was born the same year. Amma and Pitaji would call him the first Art of Living baby.

In the years that followed, the Sudarshan Kriya would become a channel for miracles in the lives of hundreds of thousands of people around the world. Many who were incapacitated were comforted, many were relieved of stress and worry, and many underwent intense mystical experiences. Some scientists were keen to understand this phenomenon. Gurudev would encourage them to do so, and eventually scientific papers were published that would prove the beneficial impact of the Kriya on the people who practised it.

Dr Fahri Saatcioglu, a professor at the University of Oslo, published the result of his research in the peer-reviewed journal *Plos One*, which describes how the Sudarshan Kriya has a rapid and significantly greater effect on gene expression compared to a controlled regimen of a walk through nature or listening to relaxing music. He writes: 'This data may be the basis for their longer term cell biological and higher level health effects.' Dr Richard Brown, associate professor of clinical psychiatry at the University of Columbia, postulated that the Sudarshan Kriya contributes to a state of alert calmness through its effect on the vagus nerve. This nerve is crucial in social bonding, empathy and love. It also impacts our perception, observation and decision-making capacity. Impaired vagal activity is found in patients of depression, anxiety, panic disorders, post-traumatic stress disorders, those with a violent streak and

RAVI AND BHANU 22-10-58

Two-and-a-half-
year-old Ravi with
baby Bhanu

Young Ravi performing aarti
in the puja room at Manjula

Young Ravi on the terrace of Manjula on his twenty-second birthday

Pitaji and Amma in the late 1950s

Young Ravi with Maharishi at the Kumbh Mela

Young Ravi with Maharishi at Seelisberg, Switzerland, in the late 1970s

Gurudev with the first batch of participants of Sudarshan Kriya in Shimoga, Karnataka, 1982

Gurudev with the first batch of Youth Leadership Training Programme participants, 1990

Gurudev with the participants of an Art of Living programme at Bishop's University, Lennoxville, Canada, 1987

Gurudev in the Narayana Hall
at the Bangalore ashram

Gurudev conducting an Art of Living programme in Montreal, Canada

Gurudev with a group of Polish participants of the first international programme conducted at the Bangalore ashram, 1991

Gurudev and Amma on a night
train from Bangalore to Solapur
along with a few volunteers, 1989

Gurudev in Hong Kong
with local volunteers and
teachers in 2004

Gurudev in Bali in the early
1990s teaching the second
Art of Living programme there

Gurudev in Slovenia

Gurudev in Lake Tahoe,
Sierra Nevada, during
Guru Purnima in the
early 1990s

Gurudev with the participants of
an advanced meditation programme
in Weggis, Switzerland

The meditation hall, Vishalakshi Mantap, at the Bangalore ashram

Shakti Kutir at the Bangalore ashram when it was just constructed, 1987

Amma with the children of the Ved
Vignan Maha Vidya Peeth free school
at the ashram campus

Satsang in the amphitheatre of the
Bangalore ashram with the Vishalakshi
Mantap in the background

Gurudev during
a US tour

Gurudev in North America
in the early 1990s

so on. Stephen W. Porges, a scientist at the Kinsey Institute and also professor of psychiatry at the University of North Carolina, further suggested that the varying rhythms of the breath in the Sudarshan Kriya stimulates different fibres of the vagus nerve creating a wide-ranging impact. Interestingly, he shared that the brain-wave patterns during and after the Kriya are similar to that of babies. Dr Patricia Gerberg from the US found the Kriya useful in healing negative past impressions in her patients undergoing psychoanalysis. So many different studies have also been conducted at the All India Institute of Medical Sciences, New Delhi. It was always exciting to see what science had to say about the Kriya—but I was certain, seeing its impact, that it is a gift to humanity.

Gurudev was constantly on the move, teaching the Kriya wherever he went. Once we were travelling to Siddhapura with him. Philip Fraser, a young American (and now a teacher with Art of Living), was also travelling with us. When we reached Shimoga, Gurudev started giving directions to the driver and we stopped in front of a small house. When Gurudev alighted from the car, the people of the house came running to him in utter disbelief and obvious gratitude. They were the participants of the very first course that Gurudev had taught in Shimoga and had been waiting to have darshan of the young saint who had transformed their lives. Gurudev, in turn, was immensely touched by their devotion and gratefulness. Years later, Fraser would recount this experience to me.

Once, we were at Pollachi, in Tamil Nadu, to visit an old saint called Koti Swami. He was believed to have lived for over four hundred years. He was thin and had long matted locks, and wore a simple orange robe. Koti Swami sat in a cane chair with his feet on a footrest. Gurudev fed the old saint himself, and he accepted every morsel with great relish. Gurudev was like a mother and the venerable old saint, a child! The holy being wanted to give something in return, too, so Gurudev asked him for knowledge. 'When Shiva himself asks for knowledge, what can I give him!' exclaimed the old soul in his ancient Tamil dialect.

Pragyanandji Maharaj was another saint who was very fond of Gurudev and liked to spend time with him. We were in Rishikesh during Ugadi (New Year as per the lunar calendar in certain parts of India) and Maharaj-ji was staying over with us. At sunrise, he came excitedly towards Gurudev's kutir, the door to which normally opened between 9.00 and 10.00 a.m. While we were at a loss regarding what to do as it was quite early in the morning, Gurudev himself came out. Maharaj-ji, without uttering a word, started prostrating himself before Gurudev, who held him as he was bowing down. The saint, in reverence, shared that he had experienced Gurudev in the form of Brahma, Vishnu and Maheshwar.

Gurudev says that divinity is present in everyone. When our body and mind are relaxed, we can discover divinity in chirping birds, rustling leaves, flowing water or tall mountains. Even erupting volcanoes, thunder and lightning, or warring human beings exude divinity—everyone has the freedom to relate to God in the form they want to. A guru is the one who kindles this awareness in us. Maharajji performed a guru puja, and all of us joined him, feeling grateful for being in the Master's presence on that special day.

These experiences gave me an inkling to my relationship with my brother—it had blossomed into an effortless bond with a Master. Earlier, I followed him without knowing and now I followed him with full knowledge. One Friday, in Manjula, he was performing a Devi puja in our small prayer room upstairs. I sat nearby in reverence to the Mother Divine. We have a small idol of Devi in our house, which we had adorned with flowers, sandal paste and kumkum. Jasmine, hibiscus, plumeria, chrysanthemum and lotus flowers, maruga and davana leaves—there was a place for each flower and leaf, both individually and collectively, in the worship of the Devi. My mother and I chanted the Lalitha Sahasranama, while my brother performed the puja. A small bell, an aarti plate with camphor, incense sticks, a small silver vessel called panchapatram filled with water, and a little spoon—these were neatly arranged in the prayer room. I would watch every delicate action of my brother with rapt attention—the way he held a flower before his heart for a fraction of a second and the way his hands flowed in a graceful arc as he offered the flower to the Devi. When one's senses are fully engaged in an act, there comes a point when the act and the actor merge into one. One becomes acutely aware of every movement and is strongly connected to everything around oneself. One becomes the flower, the chant, the fragrance, or the act. And during the puja, I had a vision of the Devi being enlivened as she rose from the idol and merged into my brother. I could hear her, the primordial energy, telling me that she and my brother were no different. The divine presence expressed itself clearly in my heart. At that moment, I recognized him as my Master.

After the puja, he gave me and my mother some water from the panchapatram as prasad. My mother tasted it and exclaimed, 'What did you mix in the water?' The water was sweet and fragrant. Today, people speak of water memory and some have studied the impact of positive vibrations on water, but in those days, these phenomena aroused pure wonder. But it was not just the water, at times the air would be infused with the fragrance of rose, jasmine or sandalwood. Whenever my brother finished a big puja or yagya, it would drizzle irrespective of the weather. Showers are considered auspicious and are an indication that nature is happy with the offerings that are made to her.

The true nature of our self is joy. Gurudev says, 'In any pleasant experience, one closes one's eyes, experiences fragrance, good taste, a gentle touch or something similar. Sukha (contentedness) is that which takes one towards the self. Dukha (suffering) is that which takes one away from the self. One suffers simply because one is caught up in an object, which keeps changing, instead of focusing on the self.'

All sense objects are just diving boards to take one back to the self. This was the journey that people undertook during their courses with Gurudev. My brother shared an anecdote related to one such course. Vishnu Bhatt was assisting him during the event.

The course was arranged at Alakananda Colony in New Delhi. Many people had come. I just sat silently through the whole course and did not utter a word. People sat waiting, five minutes, ten minutes, an hour, two hours, expecting something to happen. Everybody was experiencing something new, but Vishnu was getting nervous. He was moving, shuffling around, putting the clock in front of me, pouring water into my glass, or tapping on the microphone to see if it was working. He kept whispering 'Jai Gurudev,

Jai Gurudev.' He knew the people, had helped arrange the course, and was wondering, 'What has happened to Gurudev? He is not speaking. Time will soon run out, and the course is yet to begin!' This happened the next day as well, but the participants were undergoing a completely new experience. Once the course was over, they were crying and thanking me. Through the entire two days of the course, I did not speak a single word except at the end, when I said, 'How are you feeling now? How are you doing?' Everyone had had a life-changing experience.

Just as the earth is enlivened by the sun—even without the sun doing much—knowledge blossoms in the presence and with the grace of the Master.

8

BEYOND PRINGLES CHIPS

WHEN A GURU speaks, only wisdom springs out. But sometimes a guru does not need to even speak as his presence itself creates wisdom. As the frequency of courses increased and visitors and seekers started pouring in, my father offered to convert a small property that we owned into a place where my brother could stay and meet the people who sought his audience. We called the new place 'Gyan Mandir', which means a temple of knowledge. Every Thursday, when Gurudev was in Bangalore, he held a satsang at the place. We invited all our neighbours for the satsang. A family of two sisters and their mother would come all the way from Mysore without fail. We were a small group of eight or ten people. A spiritual guru based in Rishikesh once suggested to Gurudev, 'If you wish, thousands would come to you easily. But you would need to show some small miracle, so that they recognize there is something special.' My brother replied, 'I'm here to share wisdom, not to draw crowds.'

After about two years of travelling within India, in 1983, he travelled abroad to spread this knowledge there. He chose the UK as his first destination. When he informed us of the decision, we were concerned. Where would he stay? What will he do in the new country? He did not know anybody there and he left for the UK with just twenty dollars (that was the currency that was commonly available for international travel in those days) in hand. My mother, nevertheless, knew there was a greater purpose to his journey. She could not and would not hold him back. 'He wants to go ...', was all she said, and was soon at peace with the idea.

When he reached the UK, he was invited by an Indian astrologer to stay with him. However, it so happened that the people who came to the house were getting more interested in Gurudev than the astrologer, who was far older than Gurudev. Naturally, he felt insecure at the fact that people were seeking the advice of Gurudev, who was barely in his twenties, instead of asking for astrological readings. Finally, when he could not handle the insecurity anymore, in a spate of anger, he asked my brother to leave his house. Concerned by the astrologer's agitation—Gurudev was worried that the perturbation may affect the elderly man's health—he brought him a glass of water to drink and helped him calm down. Once the astrologer was comforted, unflurried he packed his luggage and prepared to leave. One of the regular guests at the astrologer's house had arrived at that moment. Since he had been mulling over the idea of meeting my brother again, he requested him to come home with him. Gurudev has often shared this incident as an example of holding on to one's faith, come what may. He says, 'When one is on the path of faith, one will be taken care of in every possible way. Faith is giving the divine a chance to act.'

In his subsequent trips to the UK, many who met him

experienced instances of healing. There was a small boy at the place where Gurudev was staying. The fluid in his eyes used to dry up, which restricted the movement of his eyeballs. The doctors were unable to cure him. Gurudev gave the parents a small white pearl to keep by their side as they slept and the child was cured. Hearing of this and similar such incidents of healing, people started queuing up at his door, wanting relief from various ailments. While he was not against healing physical ailments, this was not the reason why he wanted to reach out to people. He was here for those who had a real spirit of enquiry in them, for those who sought a glimpse of the infinite.

Gurudev was travelling almost ten months a year those days. He had started teaching Sudarshan Kriya in several countries outside the UK, too. The first course he conducted outside of the UK was in Montreux, Switzerland, in 1984, with just twelve people. Stella Dupuis, who had hosted him and organized the course, reminisced, 'I tried my best in what I thought should be the right way to approach an Indian guru, but he was a playful and uncomplicated soul. When I look back, I remember his joy and that everything that he looked at or touched was awashed with light.'

The following year, in the summer of 1985, he requested Ms Stella to drive along with him to Winterthur, the German part of Switzerland, to meet some people there. Although it was his and Ms Stella's first visit there, Gurudev could guide her on the way to the destination. They met two people there, one of whom, Madame Gisela, organized a course there and went on to organize many more later. He was moving from one corner of the world to another and in each place, there were people waiting for him.

When I first travelled with him outside India, in October 1989, he took me to Germany, France, Switzerland, the UK, the US and Canada. In those places, I met hundreds of people who were waiting for his arrival. In Germany, I cooked puliyogare, rasam rice and other such homely delicacies for him. He relished them and asked how I managed to prepare all that in a foreign country. I revealed that I had packed all the spices, dals and chutney powders, sufficient to last the entire journey. While I thought I had prepared well for the journey, he did not seem to think it was a good idea. 'You have to eat what is available locally. Leave all of these here. We are not carrying this with us any more.' So began my diet of fruits—big juicy grapes, more big juicy grapes, and then some. We stayed with Muriel Jagaer when we reached France. She had a three-storied house with the kitchen on the top floor. If anyone knocked at the door while we were cooking, she would open it using a remote control. That was a wonder for me! I had never seen such technology before. On the ground floor, she had a small studio with wooden floors where she practised dance. She was such a good dancer! I had only seen traditional Indian dance forms until then. When I think of her graceful movements now, I wonder if it was the dance or Muriel herself who was so beautiful. Could the dance and the dancer be separated? Gurudev says that this entire creation is the dance of the creator, who permeates each and every cell of this creation.

In between the talks and programmes, we found time for sightseeing too. We visited the Eiffel Tower and had a bird's eye view of the city from the top. One could see the way the city was neatly laid out and carefully planned. I could see hundreds of people walking and driving past, oblivious to the Master who had arrived amidst them, yet there were a few lucky ones who had found him. Was this moment—I was standing beside the Master, almost at the top of the world—planned?

Many years later, during an impromptu visit to Paris, a lady asked Gurudev, 'How did this plan for Paris come up?' He said, 'There are plans at many levels. We make plans for arranging a room—the colour to paint, where to keep the flower vase and so on. Then there are plans made for a house, street, city, or country, at various levels of detail. But the biggest of them all is that we are all here at the same time, one from Saudi Arabia, one from Germany, one from India. We are all here now. Often, things that we plan do not happen, and what seems unplanned turn out to be the real plan!' Planned or accidental, I was happy as long as I was with him. I could so easily relate to people who would, often in tears, tell me about how he appeared in their dreams or how they were waiting for him for years. It is overwhelming, and I simply wonder at his greatness and feel grateful that things have turned out the way they have.

I accompanied him to several places. Sometimes we were at temples in the UK, where he spoke to people, usually in Hindi. Although there were several local English people at those venues, it never seemed to matter what language he was speaking. Everyone was just happy to be there, soaking in his presence. One of those days, at one house, he was offered gulab jamun, a popular Indian sweetmeat. Gurudev told the lady who offered him the gulab jamuns that they were very good. Word spread of his appreciation, and from then on every hostess started serving him gulab jamuns! When we think of the gulab jamun days, we still cannot contain our laughter.

Then came the Pringles chips days when we were in the US and Canada. Wherever we went, the chips followed us. In Canada, Gurudev had a group of volunteers who with differing views would sit in his kutir and criticize each other, one at a time. Vicky Block, a volunteer from Canada, recalled this incident with fondness. She said, 'He sat in the little open loft overhead and whenever anyone's feelings seemed hurt he'd throw a Pringle over the side at them. This exercise was supposed to make them strong but perhaps it also changed the attitude towards Pringle chips forever. At one point, it was almost raining Pringles, which everyone ate while glaring at each other.' Often, we throw our judgements on people and later feel that our judgments were wrong. While we judge, we are sure about the way things are—we live in a bubble at that point of time. The Guru Tattva (the Guru Principle or the light on the wisdom in life) helps bring us out of that bubble and enlightens us on the wisdom that life offers to us. Gurudev says, 'Beyond an event, there is knowledge, beyond a person there is love, and beyond an object there is infinity'.

We gained quite a bit of knowledge from the events around Pringles chips. Once we were in an apartment in New York. Gurudev was seated on a sofa surrounded by people, who were engrossed in watching TV, as a box of Pringles was passed around. The organizer of the event, Philip Fraser, walked into the room after arranging various things related to the event. One could see he was entirely perplexed at what was happening. Gurudev was requesting somebody to surf the television channels a bit more as 'it' was going to come up.

Philip was intrigued by what 'it' meant, and finally there it was—an episode of 'I Love Lucy'. 'The enlightened Master is watching "I Love Lucy?" This was not my idea of how gurus were supposed to be.' Even as Philip was struggling to contain his excitement, he also noticed the box of Pringles that was being passed around. 'The Master eats chips too?' Having enjoyed the first episode, Gurudev announced, 'Wait! There is one more,' and the joyful exuberance continued. Philip, like most Americans, had grown up watching the show, but he had never thought that he would have an opportunity to watch it again with someone who kindled the deepest love in him. But what was even more amazing was that Gurudev never knew which channel it was on or what the schedule of programmes in New York was, yet he knew that they played back-to-back episodes. Gurudev carries the deepest wisdom with lightness, joy and innocence. You simply cannot fit the guru into a box, but all boxes fit into him!

We visited New York several times. Gurudev was invited for a talk at the United Nations headquarters during one of those visits. The night before the event, we reluctantly made our way back to bed after a joyful satsang. I was wide awake, yet it was time for rest and I got into bed. Through a skylight, I could get a glimpse of the vastness beyond. One could have conversations with the stars, the sparkling dots across the firmament. The city lights seemed to be twinkling back at them. I was enjoying the starlight when the room was suddenly bathed in brilliant light. I felt as if there was an ethereal face that peeked at me from the skylight. Certainly, it was impossible to climb up to the skylight like that! I was not experiencing any fear whatsoever but the presence of a radiant spirit. The face disappeared soon after. I could not wait to share this experience with Gurudev the next day. When I walked into his room in the morning, my brother was looking out of the window, and before I could say anything, he simply said, 'Benevolence'. Of course, he had seen the celestial being too.

We had to get ready for the talk. Although we reached on time, the hall was practically empty. There was another keynote address scheduled at the same time, and many volunteers thought that the people would have preferred to attend that programme. Gurudev, in his usual serene self, was ready to start the talk on time, but we were worried. There were still a few minutes left when one person suddenly walked in. Then another followed, and soon a large crowd poured in, so much so that even after the hall was packed, more were walking in. We had to give up our seats to accommodate the guests who had even filled up the aisles. It was a wonder how the hall had filled up so fast, but I was happy that many new people would get a chance to receive Gurudev's wisdom. The speech was fantastic and our spirits were high. One of the volunteers apprised Gurudev that a door in the corridor that led to the hall in the UN headquarters was jammed, the reason for the venue remaining empty until the last moment. As soon as the door was fixed, people started pouring in.

The intellect was satisfied with this logical explanation, but as usual there was something more to it. Gurudev said that the 'Yaksha' (guardian angel) of New York had come to visit him, too, the previous night. The Yaksha had asked what he could do for Gurudev, and my brother had told him, 'Nothing.' At the UN venue, Gurudev had remembered the Yaksha and had mentally acknowledged him. The reason why the door was fixed and for all else that unfolded at the event. Gurudev said, 'He really wanted to do something for me. Perhaps I should have asked him to help create a centre of wisdom here, a place where people could have happiness and peace of mind.' 'But who was that guardian angel?' doubts persisted in my mind. 'Angels are part of our big self,' explained Gurudev. 'The infinity assumes diverse but specific qualities, which could be called angels. Angels are nothing but rays of one's own big self and are there to serve you. Like roots, stems and leaves that sprout out of a seed, the angels manifest when one is centred. Angels rejoice in your company, but one has nothing to gain from them. They only come around to those who have nothing to gain from them. Angels are one's extended arms, and similar to the colours that constitute the sunlight, all the angels are present in one's higher self. Bliss is their breath, dispassion their abode.'

Once Gurudev was travelling to the US and was planning to stay at Wally's house, in California. An event was organized there, but Wally was a little lost, trying to set up the house— cleaning, putting on new sheets, buying new crockery and fresh flowers, and cooking food for all. One of his friends, a clairvoyant, came in a little early, wanting to help. She entered the house and was astounded. 'What's going on in your house? Have you seen the amount of light outside? Thousands of angels and beings of light are waiting outside the door. Whoever is coming must be exceptionally special.' An astrologer also turned up at the house, and everyone was enthused about his reading of Gurudev. The astrologer, happy to receive the attention, yet perplexed by what was being revealed, said, 'He has a nervous system so refined that it can cognize the entire Vedas. Normally such purity cannot handle the daily interactions of this material world. But here, the reading shows that millions and millions will come to him.' At that point, we had no inkling how soon this prediction would come to fruition.

During one of Gurudev's visits to Switzerland, there were two talks planned around the same time—one in Paris and another in Winterthur. The plan was that Gurudev would go to Paris as more people were expected there. But he chose to go to Winterthur. It turned out that there was only one person at the talk—a young Swiss schoolteacher named Marcel Verbay, who had come out of curiosity. He had never met a spiritual person before and wanted to know what it was like to meet one. What would he say? Did he even speak English, let alone French or German? Would he have some advice for me? Many questions passed through his mind as he waited for Gurudev's arrival. But Gurudev was silent, instead of talking, and at the end of the session, asked him, 'Are you happy?' And that was it.

Gautam Buddha once explained to Ananda, his disciple, how he decides on his journeys. He said, 'When I feel someone is thirsty, so thirsty that without me there is no other way for that person, I have to move in that direction.' Gurudev says, 'It is not just the Master who moves towards the disciple, but the disciple also moves towards the Master. Sooner or later they are bound to meet. The meeting is not just of the body, but of the mind, of the very soul. When two lamps are brought close to each other, the lamps remain separate but their flames merge.' Later, when asked about choosing to go to Winterthur instead of Paris, he would tell Marcel, who now followed him all over Europe, 'I came here only for you.'

I cannot stop feeling how fortunate I have been to witness the blossoming of so many hearts—like trees that open up to the breeze, the lotus to the sun, and water lilies to the moonlight, something stirs deep inside them, uncovering the mysteries of life and self. When my first trip with Gurudev was coming to a close, we were staying at a house in England. It was bedtime, and most had retired to their rooms. Some of my luggage was left downstairs, and I had to carry them up. As I was coming down, I slipped, tumbled down the flight of stairs, and landed with a thud. I was hurting badly and was not sure if I could move. Gurudev rushed out of his room, asking if I was okay. Although I told him I was fine, I had no clue as to how my body was faring.

It is important what one speaks in front of one's guru. While on the one hand, one is an open book with nothing to hide, on the other, when one's guru asks how things are, only positive words tumble out of one's mouth. I got up with some help, bore the pain, and somehow managed to bide the time before I reached home. I could have seriously hurt myself, considering the impact of the fall, but somehow I managed to escape intact. There is a proverb in Kannada, which could be roughly translated as, 'What came for the head left with the headgear.'

Once I was home, Pitaji was utterly relieved. Being an astrologer, he knew that it was a bad period for me, but had never shared this with any of us as he knew Gurudev would take care of me and was happy that I was with him. The supposed 'bad period' turned out to be a magical journey for me.

9

AMIDST THE FIVE HILLOCKS

LOOKING OUT OF my window in California now, I see birds returning to their nests. How organized they are, and always together. While flying they give each other so much space: they never collide with one another or cause confusion. Gurudev says, 'Like birds returning to their nests, keep coming back to your source. You would then realize that you host the divine too.' From this fast-paced world, people keep coming back to the ashram, into its loving fold, making a journey back to their home, their source.

At Manjula, our home, discussions around the need for an ashram kept coming up. Gurudev agreed to the idea when he felt that the time was right. One day, we packed ourselves into our father's white Ambassador and set off on a drive to search for an ideal spot for the ashram. We drove towards south Bangalore, which was yet to be urbanized, along Kanakapura Road, which was lined on both sides by huge, beautiful trees. The trees formed an enchanting canopy over us. Ours was the only vehicle on the road, which was bordered by woods. Wild elephants and other animals freely roamed about in the area. We would have driven about thirteen kilometres when Gurudev asked my father to stop the car. To our right we could see some hillocks—bare and reddish in hue. We alighted and followed Gurudev on foot towards them. He took a few steps and said, 'This is it.'

My father filed an application with the government for procuring the land. A few days later, one of our acquaintances came home excited. He had driven past the area with a famous astrologer who had pointed out at the land and said, 'The one who owns this land would have a profound impact on the world.' While such predictions were always good to hear, bribes were demanded for sanctioning the land. Pitaji was not prepared to pay even a dime as bribe as he was a true Gandhian. As a result, we ended up spending hours waiting at the land registrar's office. There were times when even my children accompanied me as we waited. I would pack snacks for them and make them feel as if we were on a picnic at the Vidhana Soudha, where the offices of the legislative assembly were located. But even after many hours of waiting, little progress was being made. Pitaji would say, we will keep going back and do it the right way even if it takes a long time. Perhaps, seeing how determined Pitaji was, the officials finally allotted the land to us.

Once the land was procured, the first task was performing the bhumi puja. Five women, including my mother and I, performed the puja. Soon after the ceremony, Gurudev chose a spot and said, 'Drill a bore well here.' Pitaji brought some workmen and immediately set himself to the task. The ground was rocky and although they were disappointed initially with the results, they did not give up. At around

2 a.m. in the morning, water came gushing out, much to the joy of everybody. This well is a source of water for the entire ashram even today. We never engaged the services of a water diviner. Gurudev would just walk across the land and find water sources. Once, he even chose a spot close to the top of one of the hillocks. Though perplexed by this choice, once the spot was drilled, we were greeted by a spring of water. There was an instance when another Swamiji, whose ashram was about a few kilometres away from ours, requested Gurudev's help for locating water. The people at the ashram had drilled about twenty-one spots with no success. Gurudev went to the ashram and solved the issue with ease!

Today, inspired by him, Art of Living volunteers have rejuvenated about thirty rivers, and water flows in areas that have remained dry for decades. One of the volunteers shared that she was amazed at the result of their efforts. They would just take Gurudev's name and begin the work, and where science failed to find solutions, faith would work. Sometimes I wonder whether he knew where the water was flowing or water flowed where he wanted it to flow. This difference perhaps exists only at a rational level, but when one is connected with creation, there is perfect harmony between oneself and nature. Nature supports one fully and one is completely aligned with her.

Once the bore wells were drilled, a cottage was set up with mud floors and a thatched roof held up by bamboo poles. It was called Shakti. Gurudev stayed in this simple cottage, which leaked during the rains. There was very little by way of physical comfort in the ashram at that time. Still, a few volunteers, who came from different parts of the country and across the world, made it their home. Two sets of kutirs, called Vasistha and Vishwamitra, were the first blocks to come up. They were low-cost stone structures decorated with delicate lotus petal designs along the borders—the petals were Gurudev's idea. A little ahead of the first cottage, we built a small round kutir for Gurudev, which had a hat-shaped cemented mesh roof. This became the Shakti Kutir eventually and the other cottage was renamed Narayana, which became a venue for various courses, pujas and satsangs.

When Gurudev shared his intention of training people so that they could teach the Sudarshan Kriya to others, a lot of people were uncertain. When he announced that he would make a tape of the Kriya to teach others, many thought that it might not work. Christopher Kiran Byrt, a volunteer from Germany, was initially hesitant but came around to the idea. He reminisced, 'How could one possibly record something so alive, subtle and profound on a tape? Still, a tape recorder and microphone were arranged and we started the process. For over twenty years since then, the same recording was used to teach the Sudarshan Kriya around the world. Many will remember the sounds of a squeaking gate, barking dogs and honking buses that drove down the Kanakapura Road which became part of the recording. Little did we realize that history was in the making. A beautiful picture of Gurudev from his trip to Solapur was made the cover of the Kriya tape. Technological changes have resulted in the Kriya now being available on mobile devices, but the tape was and still is the most valuable and sacrosanct possession of most Art of Living teachers. The number of courses and participants kept increasing and the construction work was continued to accommodate the steadily growing numbers.

While the construction was going on, the children of the construction workers played around the ashram without going to school. Their parents had never been to school and had no such plans for the children either. Gurudev asked a few volunteers at the ashram to get the children together and teach them personal hygiene along with reading and writing skills. Initially, there were about thirty odd children. Pitaji went around nearby villages and convinced more families to send their children to the ashram to be educated. In the beginning, the free and nutritious midday meal was the chief attraction but, with time, as parents started seeing positive results in their children, they took pride in getting them educated. Thirty grew to over two thousand children in just a few years.

Along with the construction activities, the other main task was planting saplings in the rocky landscape of the ashram. Watering saplings was a very important seva activity for ashram members. There were no garden hoses or multiple water pipes. Water would have to be filled and carried to each of the saplings bucket by bucket. Sometimes a human chain would be formed to pass the buckets all the way to the saplings, which consumed a couple of hours each day. Often the volunteers would check with Gurudev to see if it would rain that day, so that they could decide on whether to water the saplings or not.

Whenever Gurudev returned from his tours, he would walk around the ashram checking on the plants and trees. And if it was found that even one plant was not watered by mistake, he ensured that it was immediately taken care of. I have myself planted and nurtured so many plants and trees in the ashram. Jasmines, red hibiscuses, anthuriums, cannonball trees—it is said that cannonball trees, known also as nagalinga trees, do not grow everywhere and take several years to blossom. But in the ashram, not only did they grow sturdy and tall but also blossomed in less than five years. I had grown over five hundred varieties of crotons in Manjula and sent their cuttings to the ashram. The gardeners grew the crotons across the ashram and soon most of them reached almost my height! I made trips to Lalbagh to meet forest officers and learn about new plants. I researched on plants that attracted various kinds of birds and butterflies. But after all the discussions, I could not get hold of most of the plants as they were too expensive and we had a limited budget. But then somehow someone would drop by with the kind of plant I wanted, and I would carefully plant those saplings in select locations around Gurudev's kutir and across the ashram. Over the years, the rocky red earth of the ashram transformed into a lush green haven for all sorts of flora and fauna. The way these saplings, nourished by water and sun, grew stronger by the day, the seeds of love and wisdom sown in the hearts of the volunteers were also nourished by their sadhana or spiritual practices.

One day Gurudev requested one of our volunteers, Kiran, to pick up the sapling of a banyan tree and follow him. He walked up a hillock to a specific spot and said, 'Plant it here.' Once the sapling was planted he said, 'One day, there will be a hall here and we will sit under this tree and have beautiful satsangs.' That day was not too far. The spot was the highest point of one of the hillocks, where an open-air hall was built. Each of the pillars of the hall is associated with a certain zodiac sign. As the sun moves through the zodiacs, its rays fall on the pillar associated with a specific sign. If the sun was in Leo, it would shine on the pillar that had the zodiac Leo carved on it. Gurudev called it the Sumeru Mantap. Several years later, when I travelled to Peru with Gurudev, we visited Machu Picchu. At the historic ruins there, people spoke of a construction based on the movement of the sun through the zodiac signs. Although Mayan architects had come up with such a wonderful concept many aeons ago, the science behind it was almost unknown to us. Gurudev says that knowledge is structured in our consciousness. There is so much intelligence in creation that if our mind were to be aligned with it, the intelligence would become available to us. In a sense, nothing is ever lost.

The Sumeru Mantap has been the site of some of the most magical satsangs at the ashram. Gurudev would be seated on a single stone bench right below the magnificent banyan tree that had grown enough to stretch its arms and capture a sliver of the sky above the Mantap. A palm leaf reader who once visited us said that the Mantap was a sacred place and that it was where the Divine Mother chose to rest with her retinue after vanquishing Mahishasura. A similar reading mentioned the existence of a Shiva temple right below where the Shakti Kutir was located and a Devi temple submerged under the lake that is adjacent to the ashram. Just below the Mantap, a simple meditation hall with an arched roof was constructed. Gurudev insisted on a translucent blue roof for the hall. When people opened their eyes after a deep meditation, he wanted them to feel that they were gazing into the sky—a continuum of the boundless space that they had experienced within themselves. Judy, a devotee from England, even painted puffy clouds on the blue canvas sheet with which the roof was covered.

Pitaji consulted Gurudev on every aspect of the construction that was going on in the initial days. Everything was designed in an eco-friendly and cost-effective way. Still, we had to face resistance from villagers from time to time. Once they even turned up with burning torches. Gurudev was away on tour, but Pitaji somehow managed to mollify the angry villagers.

When Gurudev travelled, he called Pitaji every day at around 9 p.m., and Pitaji updated him on the day-to-day events at the ashram. One day, Gurudev called a little earlier than usual, at around 8.30 p.m, but Pitaji was busy freshening up at that time. Gurudev told my mother that he would call them after they had had their dinner. 'No no, Pitaji will eat only after he speaks to you. Call back soon,' Amma insisted. Talking to his son was as sacred as any puja for my father.

Puja is a Sanskrit word that means 'born out of fullness or gratefulness'. Prayer could be an expression of our gratitude or it could arise out of helplessness. We were once travelling with Gurudev in Assam. While driving through a forest, at one point he instructed the driver to turn away from the main road and take an unchartered course. A little later, we stopped at a clearing outside a small hut. Vinod Menon, a young devotee from Kerala, was travelling along with us. Gurudev asked him how much money he had with him. Vinod had close to seven hundred and fifty rupees. Gurudev requested him to give the money to the woman in the hut. When Vinod returned, the woman, in tears, came out with him. She was a simple tribal woman, whose husband was seriously ill. She had been praying to God to send her some help, and Vinod had given her just the right amount to buy the necessary medicines. She lived in a humble one-room hut, the walls of which were adorned with pictures of Mother Divine and Sri Ramakrishna Paramahamsa, the famous mystic and yogi. She had been crying in front of the pictures, praying for help. When we left from there, Gurudev explained how her prayer had pulled him. 'But she had been praying to the Mother Divine and to Sri Ramakrishna—how did Gurudev manage to overhear it?' we asked incredulously. 'All calls come on the same line,' pat came the reply.

There were no telephones at the ashram in those days. But sometimes some people at the ashram felt that Gurudev was calling out to them and would come running to Shakti Kutir. They would find others, too, who had had the same feeling, standing outside the kutir. Gurudev would emerge from the kutir and say, 'Ah! You have come ...,' and would proceed to convey his message.

Gurudev would rest briefly in the afternoons. Once, I was reading Yoga Vasishta (a dialogue between Lord Rama and Sage Vasishta on the nature of the true self, creation) to him as he was resting. As I heard a gentle snore, I stopped reading. But immediately, the snoring stopped and I had to resume my reading. This happened several times. When Gurudev woke up, he said, 'You should not stop in the middle of a reading. Even if I seem to be sleeping, I am listening. This is called listening with the sixth sense.' Many a time, he has been able to recollect chapters that were read during his sleep and even speak about them during satsangs.

There is a small portico outside Shakti Kutir. Gurudev would be seated there on a simple chair, and the rest of us would sit around him on the tiled floor. He would smile in silence, twirl his mala between his fingers, and look into space or at us. Sometimes, we sang as he sat facing the moon; at other times, he would speak a few words. One such evening, out of the blue, he said, '*Anuttaro Bhava* ...' (be answerless) with no further explanation. About twenty years later, when he was speaking on the Vijnana Bhairava Tantra, the same phrase came up. 'So this is where it came from,' he said as if the whole episode happened just a few moments ago! There was a continuum to everything that he did. When one looks back, it is easier to connect the dots, but when one is immersed in the moment, one realizes that everything is available at that particular moment!

The little portico outside Shakti Kutir has been the stage for innumerable such moments. Once, a group of international guests had come to visit the ashram. They had come to meet spiritual gurus in India as they wanted to witness some miracles. It was a lovely evening with a pleasant breeze around the ashram and an ideal time for a light snack. Gurudev asked them about their favourite fruits. Some said strawberries, others mangosteen, and yet others nectarine—fruits that were relatively unheard of in India at that time. Gurudev went inside the Kutir and came out a little later holding a platter of neatly cut fruits. It had all the types of fruits that were mentioned. The guests were taken aback. Gurudev smiled and encouraged them to taste the fruits. They relished the fruits so much that some said they would not find such succulent fruits even back in their homeland where they grew in abundance. After giving them this little surprise, Gurudev gently told them, 'Do not go to spiritual gurus for miracles. Go to them seeking wisdom.'

When there is faith, miracles do happen. Just outside Shakti Kutir, Gurudev sometimes sits on a small wooden chair which has coir matting. One evening, seated there and gazing into the sky, he said, 'Tomorrow there will be a miracle.' One could expect such a statement to attract hundreds of questions and demands for further explanations. But when the Master speaks, one has faith and is open to all possibilities. The next day, as dawn broke, news of Ganesha idols drinking milk started pouring in from different parts of the world. There was a small Ganesha idol close to the entrance of the ashram, and when we offered it milk, the milk disappeared into its trunk. When Gurudev was informed of this, he said, 'Such miracles happen from time to time to restore faith in a higher power.' During the satsang conducted that evening, Gurudev spoke of the presence of innumerable angels amidst us.

A few years later, a devotee from Taiwan clicked pictures during one of the satsangs with a Polaroid camera, but the photographs were filled with hundreds of little circular blobs of light. Who would have thought that the divine beings would be kind enough to show up on ordinary photographs. For a long time after this, people were engrossed in clicking photos of not only the people and objects in the ashram, but of empty spaces too!

'When one buys a tea cup, does one pay for the cup or the space that it encloses? If the same material were to be rolled into the shape of a ball, would one pay for it too?' Gurudev once asked. It was a new way of looking at things. The mind is used to duality and is often at wonder regarding what to say. But spirituality is never exclusive and there are no conflicts. Seekers for centuries have debated over the virtues of the manifest and the unmanifest, the tangible and the intangible. But Gurudev has always emphasized upon the middle path by honouring every aspect of our existence, including our body and spirit, the form and the formless. As a child, he was engrossed in worshipping idols, but as a teenager, he moved on to honouring the formless, too, and Vedic chants gained in importance. Eventually, I saw him spending hours and, sometimes days together, in silence and meditation. Today, we enjoy pujas accompanied by the mystical sounds of ancient chants and slip effortlessly into meditation in his presence.

Gurudev says, 'Harmony in movement is dance. Harmony in sound is music. Harmony in mind is meditation and in life it is celebration.' The satsang conducted every evening at the ashram consists of dance, music, meditation, and is a celebration of life. People usually practise for hours before they are confident of singing in tune or being heard in public. But during the satsang, songs and poems flow out of people as naturally as a waterfall. Whether one is a good singer or not does not matter, people just sing their hearts out. Of course, many sing out of key and often they tend to be the loudest, but when every heart unites in the act of singing, a pleasant wave of positivity sweeps across the participants. One is part of an expanding field of compassionate energy emanating from the Master. Pain disappears into oblivion, and one feels refreshed and light.

Once, a few days after Shivaratri, Gurudev was getting ready for a tour abroad. He was travelling light, but just the thought of my brother being away made me teary-eyed. Sniffling, I was sitting at the back seat of the car en route to the airport, and Gurudev suddenly said, 'Bhanu, listen to a new song', and in the most mellifluous voice he sang, '*Shivoham, shivoham, shivaswaroopoham ... Nithyoham, shuddhoham, buddhoham, muktoham ...'* Suddenly, there was a paradigm shift in my state of being. I was all ears, absorbing every word and music into me, and the crying stopped. Gurudev boarded his flight, and I kept humming the song until I reached home. I did not stop lest I forgot the song! I sang it to Amma as well to ensure that between us we would remember the song correctly. There were no cell phones in those days and I was not even carrying a pen or paper. Gurudev had said I should sing the song once he was back from the tour. We kept practising the song, and when he arrived many months later, he sang the whole song during a satsang. He had not forgotten a word, and I realized that he was successful in keeping my mind engaged during his absence.

In the ashram, one is happy being busy and busy being happy. Sadhana, seva and satsangs are a part of our daily routine at the ashram. Sunrise is the time for sadhana, which includes some yoga, Sudarshan Kriya and meditation. Breakfast is followed by seva, which includes gardening, cleaning and helping in the kitchen. Almost everybody who comes to the ashram has had the experience of peeling and chopping mountains of potatoes and carrots even if they had never held a kitchen knife in their life! Often 'novices' could be seen taking guidance from 'experts' and an in-depth conversation about the fastest ways to peel and chop vegetables would ensue. Slowly, as one settles into the act of chopping, the mind also settles, and there comes a point when the act becomes effortless. The act simply happens and the actor merely turns into a witness. 'You are made up of the carrots and potatoes that you eat. Have you thought of this?' my brother asked me once. Voila! And a deeper connection with vegetables emerged. While we dwelt on what we were made of, Amma was mostly involved in the more prosaic act of thinking whether potatoes were cheaper compared with pumpkins on a particular day. She was careful about every rupee that was spent and was not only involved in buying vegetables and provisions but also estimating which shop was cheaper. Bit by bit she saved, so that the money could be channelized into serving society. The ideal that she set for the ashram still continues to be its leading light.

But her prudence with money was not evident in the atmosphere of abundance that always surrounded her. Amma's kitchen buzzed with activity through the day. Everyone was welcome and was fed with tasty food prepared by Amma herself. For Gurudev, she would pack food with a dozen different accompaniments and at least four different chutneys! Some days, I would come to the ashram with the food but would forget to open one of the small boxes of accompaniments. He would not only point it out to me, but also make it a point to tell my mother. And my mother would say, 'She doesn't know to cook and can't serve also!' Many a time, Gurudev helped her in the kitchen and prepared a surprise dish that would be lovingly served to everybody. Once, in Japan, we reached our host's house with a group of about fifty people at around lunch time. The hosts, however, were caught off guard as they were expecting just five to six people. But Gurudev started serving what was available, and everybody had their fill! When he would come to Manjula for Devi puja on Fridays, it was difficult to assess how many people to cook for. There were instances when three hundred people ate from food that was prepared for just seventy or eighty.

In 1999, we organized an Anandotsav (celebration of joy) in which several hundred people participated. I was in the kitchen cooking for the guests and ended up making over 4500 aloo bondas. One person was making the potato balls, another was dipping them in the batter, and I was frying them. Since then, I have always had a good cook at home. Gurudev says, 'You are doing my work and I am taking care of you.' Having a kitchen help even in our small house is really a gift.

Once, a large group from an institution was visiting the ashram, but the cook at the ashram was on leave. I rushed to the ashram with Shailaja Kulkarni, one of the volunteers. We first cleaned the vessels and were sweeping the kitchen when the cook from the said institution walked in. He asked if I worked at the ashram and wanted to know the salary I was being paid. I said, 'No salary, I am here to do seva.' 'It is the same for me. I get one rupee as a token amount,' he said. Later in the afternoon, when they were having lunch, the head of the group praised the food. They enjoyed the upma, sambar, palya and curd rice that was served. 'Bhanu, my sister, did the cooking today,' Gurudev told them and introduced me. The cook who was present at the lunch felt very embarrassed at this and wanted to apologise to me, but the whole affair ended up in laughter.

The visitors then invited us over to their campus, and I was given a walk-through of their kitchen, which had several machines for cooking purposes. Today, I feel proud when I think of the chapati-making machines in our kitchen that make about 2000 chapatis every minute! The ashram kitchen feeds over 10,000 people each day. The number of people has varied, the kitchen location has changed, the facilities have improved, and even the sevaks are different now, but the mountains of potatoes and carrots continue.

As the number of participants kept increasing, Gurudev had a vision for a meditation hall to be built at the ashram. A few of us were with him when he took out a piece of paper and started sketching a design for the hall, which resembled a fully blossomed lotus flower. Manu Makhija from Hong Kong requested with great love and humility for an opportunity to build the hall and Gurudev readily agreed. As the hall started coming up, a name had to be chosen, and Manu suggested that the hall be named after Amma—as Vishalakshi Mantap. I loved the idea and Gurudev accepted it too. 'Vishal' means broad and 'aksh' means eyes. Vishalakshi is the one with a broad vision, an all-inclusive sense of belongingness. For every pillar that was constructed, a home was donated to the homeless in nearby villages. Many people came forward to be part of the construction efforts. On 18 January 2003, the Vishalakshi Mantap was inaugurated. Although it was the biggest hall in the ashram at that time, it was filled to capacity with people having to wait outside. Over the past many years, millions have meditated and experienced the depth of their being in this monument of love and labour. Many have asked Gurudev, 'How can I know you fully?' He would say, 'First know yourself, then you would realize that there is no you and me, and that you are nothing but me'.

10

SLEEPLESS NIGHTS UNDER
THE EASTERN SKIES

THE NIGHT SKY is filled with a million sparkling stars. They twinkle and pulsate in far-off skies and are visible only in the absence of the sun. One runs behind stars only when one is oblivious to the sun, which is one's own self. In the silence of the night, as the mind becomes still, little rays of starlight remind one of the glory of our effulgent self.

Once people participated in the two-day programme and had learnt the Sudarshan Kriya, they could attend an 'advanced programme', which was a residential silence programme that lasted anywhere between seven and fifteen days. Gurudev would conduct meditations, which he would refer to as 'hollow and empty' to indicate the phenomenal expansion of the consciousness. He would guide us step by step into the realms of the unknown, which is inexpressible, and the unbounded divinity within us. The soft and melodic nature of his instructions, the mesmerizing shlokas at the end ... words cannot possibly explain how deep and profound the experience was.

The first advanced meditation programme was conducted in Vasanthapura, Bangalore, in 1988. Eighty-one participants from thirteen countries realized and soaked in the depth of their blissful selves in the presence of the Master. The subsequent courses were conducted at the ashram. The very first programme organized at the ashram was for a Polish group. Gurudev had a penchant for giving unique names to the courses: Wisdom of Fools, Ancient Love, Sound of Sandals, Unpushed Button, Sleepless Nights under the Eastern Skies, and so on.

I participated in one of the ten-day advanced meditation programmes conducted in Kolkata. During the course, Gurudev beckoned me to come forward and have a look at the people in the hall. He asked me if I could accept everyone as my own children. Now this was a little comical as almost everyone in the group was older to me. Besides, it was easier to be closer to children, and I was not even remotely connected to the people present there. But Gurudev instructed me to close my eyes and a process of reorientation began. After a few seconds, I opened my eyes, and he asked me again. 'Could you be a mother to all?' Suddenly, something in my heart exploded, and I felt as if I was radiating love. I started looking at the people assembled in the hall as small children. 'How could I even think of not loving them?' I thought, and tears started flowing from my eyes. Ego is a barrier, and only a master can help one deal with it and transcend it.

There was another special ten-day programme that he called the 'Danda' course. As the name suggests, we were each given a 'danda' or a piece of stick, which we had to hold on to for ten days. The stick was like an extension of our body.

Just like how it is impossible to leave one's hand behind, one cannot be separated from one's danda. The experience that we had with the course was indescribable. Gurudev said, 'The Brahmadanda brings balance between both worlds and is a connection to this world. When you take it along with you, there is just one responsibility and awareness. Even a sanyasi does not get a danda immediately; one has to have a guru to get it.' At the end of the programme, when I had to return my danda to Gurudev, I was in tears. But they were tears of love, not of sadness. He has so far conducted three Danda courses, and perhaps the time will come for another one soon.

Gurudev often speaks of the meditation programme as a journey from the head to the heart. The path is exciting! Small things reveal unforeseen depths. Sometimes, lunch comprised just a juicy grapefruit with instructions to taste and savour the fruit for a few minutes by relating to it completely in terms of its essence, temperature and texture. By devoting our attention to a grape absolutely, we could reach a deep meditative state. During a course that he taught at Ooty, Tamil Nadu, participants had to walk as fast as they could, or even run, through a natural tunnel that connected the two hotels where they were staying in. Participants who attempted it came out of the tunnel feeling relaxed and light. Many shared that they felt freedom from fear. Of course, one could have walked through that tunnel or have grapefruits a dozen times without feeling any difference whatsoever. The technique is as essential as is the presence of a master for transforming such humdrum activities into enthralling experiences. There have been several such activities through which hundreds of thousands of people have had life-changing experiences.

In the US, advanced courses were initially held at facilities usually allotted for summer camps, such as Camp Whittier and Camp Universe, which had just basic accommodation with bunk beds, central washing areas and the like. For us, though, comfort meant how much time we got to spend with Gurudev. During one such trip, he was invited for a talk organized at the grand suite of a plush hotel. We were with him, too, and this time was no different. He was absolutely at home whether he was resting on the wooden bunk bed at Camp Whittier or at a posh suite.

During an advanced course given at Timmendorfer Strand, North Germany, Gurudev asked us to gaze at the stars if we could find any. I had to search hard and could find only one. But after a quick spell of meditation, I opened my eyes to see the sky full of stars. Not that they were not there earlier, but it was just that our vision had opened up with more clarity. Life offers everything to us, but it is important to have a clear vision to perceive it. At the end of a period of silence during the course, Gurudev, referring to the then divided Germany, said, 'Your silence and meditation will help bring the wall down.' Kiran, who was part of the group, later shared how it sounded impossible to him then despite being tremendously touched by the idea. He, similar to many others who were part of the course, had grown up in a divided Germany, and anyone who said that the wall would come down was considered a dreamer at best. However, within a year, they saw the wall coming down and Germany moving towards the path of reunification.

The advanced programme has seen many walls and barriers breaking down, especially between people, faiths and nations.

Among the multitude of identities and labels that we don, the greatest is our identity as a human being. Spirituality unites people at the level of bare humanity, helping dissolve differences. I have seen people from Israel and Palestine, India and Pakistan, Armenia and Azerbaijan coming together and joining hands in a spirit of celebration and unity, pledging to help bring peace to their people. Many who were affected by the traumas of violence and wars have gained a new lease of life through the programme. One such instance took place at an advanced course in Rishikesh, India. Gurudev was keen on bringing peace to a region in Bihar that was afflicted with Maoist violence. Sanjay Kumar, a young and dynamic Art of Living teacher, was sent to the area. He initiated a dialogue between two major warring factions and jump-started various relief programmes. Gurudev suggested that the leaders of the warring factions be requested to come to Rishikesh. Normally, members of such factions would neither prefer to come out of their hiding nor would they meet eye to eye. However, heeding Gurudev's advice, they decided to take the bold step of visiting Rishikesh. But there was a catch—neither of the factions was in the know regarding the other coming to Rishikesh. As expected, both confronted each other at the railway station, and but for the presence and intervention of Sanjay, the groups, armed to the teeth, would have caused great damage if not outright bloodshed at the station. However, somehow they were persuaded to still travel to Rishikesh, and upon their arrival, Gurudev spoke to them, spent time with them, and managed to teach them the art of meditation. During the first few days, they came armed to the sessions, but within three days, they were relaxed and started participating in the programme, singing together. On the last day of the programme, Gurudev garlanded both the leaders, and they embraced each other and promised to put an end to the violence. It was a historic event that ended years of animosity and restored peace and joy in the area. Gurudev advised them to nourish the newfound peace by way of organizing satsangs and preeti bhoj—where the two communities would cook and eat together.

There was a similar instance, this time in a village in France. Gurudev arrived at the village, greeted enthusiastically by the participants. The village was located outside of Paris in an area surrounded by castles. Though the area was picturesque, its atmosphere was heavy. Gurudev said that this was due to past violence there. On the last afternoon of the course he said:

> All the meditations, chantings and Kriya have been beneficial for the whole area. You have managed to clear the area of its heaviness and the whole atmosphere has become calmer. When a nuclear bomb explodes, it creates radiation, and that radiation stays for a long time. Violence, anger, jealousy, the negative effects of war and crime—they irradiate the environment. To clear those effects, we would have to meditate and do the Kriya several times. That is why, albeit the course being very short, we have in many ways succeeded in doing some good for this village. This will also reduce the distress of the people and increase their well-being. You have done a great service by participating in this programme. Take it that way. That is the truth.

Back in Paris one more satsang was conducted where Gurudev taught everyone a new song of Shiva that brought up the energy of the room many notches. Singing the song felt like floating above the great Himalayas calling out to Shiva. The melody of the song reverberated across countries as it was carried across North America as well when Gurudev toured the continent. Gurudev was constantly on the move helping people experience an unchanging truth. He was invited for a dialogue on spirituality at the Berkeley Divinity School at Yale in April 1990, where he was introduced as a treasure of India. The large seminary was filled beyond capacity and additional video monitors had to be set up outside to enable the crowd to watch the programme. Abbot Thomas Keating, a founder of Centering Prayer, a popular Christian meditation method, was also on the panel. The high point of the evening came during a discussion on what a spiritual journey meant. Where does it start? Gurudev responded by sharing a poem that he penned at the venue:

Don't move an inch
The journey has begun
If you move, you are light years away
Neither East nor West
Nor North nor South

Don't move an inch.

Between the earth and the sky
The goal dawns on you
Don't move an inch.
Worms move through books and
Birds sing His songs
Don't move an inch.

Fill the lobbies of logic
With the smoke of His presence
Don't move an inch

The roof is on
With a billion stars
The sun and the moon
Moving around you
Don't move an inch.

Don't move an inch
So that waves of love
May arise in your heart
And rock your life in total bliss
I am the path, the goal, and the seeker
Don't move an inch.

Who should not move? Should the body be still, or the mind? Even as one ponders upon this and slips into meditation, one gets a glimpse of something that is beyond these dualities.

11

WHISPERING INFINITY

IN THE CALM sea ahead of me, there are a few boats speeding in various directions, entertaining the riders and onlookers alike. In life, many of our thoughts are such—they have just entertainment value. But I feel deeply in love with the divinity that has created me and everything around me. I am grateful that I do not wander aimlessly and am blessed that I am close to the Master.

Almost everyone who comes to Gurudev feels grateful, and when they ask him what they can do to spread his message, he says, 'Spread the wisdom and share this joy. Bring the light to others.' But how would anyone else spread the message as well as he could? He says, 'You are walking this path. I am just asking you to hold a few more hands and walk. I am here to take you to the goal.' He has, for instance, designed a teacher's training programme (TTP). While it is an intense programme for aspiring teachers, the training continues even after the programme in an informal manner. There are many qualities that Gurudev fosters and have taught by example. He once had to travel to Hubli, Karnataka, for a programme. The next morning, he was busy cleaning up the room where he had stayed overnight. To the volunteers who took exception to this, he said, 'We should always leave a place better than how we found it.'

One day, Bharat Shirur, now Swami Brahmatej, an Art of Living teacher with over two decades of experience, told Gurudev, 'You should scold me once in a while. That way I can make sure that I am disciplined in my practice.' Gurudev was looking into the mirror, about to apply sandalwood paste on his forehead, but turned back and said, 'You are trying to change my nature? You change! It is not in my nature to scold anybody, is it?' Bharat immediately realized that he needed to take responsibility for his own self.

I had a family to take care of and, as a result, would, at times, fail to devote as much time in ashram seva as I wanted to. One day, I was thinking about this as I entered Gurudev's room, but before I could say anything, he looked at me and said, 'No complaints, and no excuses.' His words have since then helped me mould my attitude towards my life for the better. Being an Art of Living teacher is not just about playing a set role for a few hours but is about integrating those learnings into one's life.

Gurudev taught me to see the divine in my children. Feeding them was feeding the divine, playing with them was playing with the divine, and bringing them up was ananda yog (yoga of bliss) and not a tiresome responsibility. He taught me to see the best qualities in people and nurture them further. He never made anyone feel guilty. If one bites the tongue by mistake, the teeth responsible cannot be held guilty as they are part and parcel of one's being. Teachers are a part of Gurudev's being, and ignorance of this fact could make one feel disconnected.

The seat of a guru is called Vyasa Peeta. The moment one takes that seat, a higher connection is established. Knowledge flows through oneself, and when one speaks and listens, one is amazed at the words, solutions and answers that flow out. Once, during an advanced programme, a participant asked Gurudev a question before hastily adding, 'Please think about my question and only then answer.' Gurudev said, 'I never think before I speak. I only say what the consciousness wants me to speak at any given moment.' All your life you are told to think before you speak and here is someone who says 'I never think before I speak.' Yet, his answers are perfect solutions to one's problems. When one watches this happening, the presence of a higher cosmic intelligence is very palpable. Further, he has been generous enough to share his experiences with every Art of Living teacher. Gurudev has often said, 'The guru is not just a body but a tattva—a principle, an energy—that is all pervading, similar to the self. Honouring the guru is, therefore, honouring one's self.'

Once, in the late 1980s, Gurudev gave me instructions to initiate Khurshed Batliwala and Rajesh Krishnamurthy, two young college boys, into meditation. They were my first students. Once they received the mantra, they started meditating and soon were in a deep trance. Minutes passed by, but they continued to be in that profound state of meditative consciousness. I waited for them to open their eyes but to no avail. After about forty-five minutes, I started whispering, 'Jai Gurudev' in the hope that they would regain awareness of their surroundings. Gradually, they opened their eyes and shared that they did not realize how much time had passed. The Guru Mantra is so powerful that it connects one to the deepest layers of one's consciousness. There are numerous mantras and mediation techniques now available on the internet, but the reality is that only a lit candle can light another. Only an enlightened master could bring transformation to one's life. This is why in the past, a person without a guru was called 'anatha', meaning, without a Lord or a guide, or helpless.

I have been fortunate enough to teach the art of meditation to thousands of people across the world. When they open their eyes after experiencing meditation, there is a gentle smile, a sweet tear of gratitude, and a sense that they have just experienced something deeply profound. Seeing this is the greatest fulfillment for me. Once, a gentleman, overwhelmed with tears of gratitude, told Gurudev, 'You are a roof to my life, protecting me from the sun and rain.' Gurudev replied, 'Not a roof, but an umbrella. I will be with you everywhere you go!'

I was once at Apple Valley, California, with Gurudev. He was to go for a talk and left a little earlier than usual. I was to drive down later with our host, Nirmala, who was about five months pregnant at that time. She drove slowly and carefully. But soon night fell, and we thought it would be better if we drove a little faster. At one point, the signboard on the roadside pointed towards the right, but when we turned right, we drove straight onto a culvert. Nirmala applied the brakes with all her strength and the car shrieked to a stop with its front tyres rising off the ground and the base getting stuck in the culvert. We got off from the car feeling thankful that neither of us was hurt but were shaken by the episode. Soon help arrived, and we reached our destination safe and sound. Somehow, the sign board had come unhinged, and as a result the arrow pointed towards the right instead of the road to the left. People were waiting for us worried as if they were in the know that something bad could happen. They informed us that Gurudev had been asking about me constantly. 'Where is Bhanu? Where have they reached?' At one point he had even got up from his seat concerned and said, 'If anything happens to Bhanu, I will stop teaching.' I went to Gurudev and informed him of the accident and that everything was now under control. When we passed the site the next morning, we saw that not far from the culvert, there was a deep chasm. But for the culvert, the accident could have been fatal.

In another instance, Marcy, a Canadian, had organized a programme for Gurudev in the city of Iqaluit, which is known for its polar climate. He went there on a chartered plane with five others. They were received by the local Inuit chief, who told Gurudev, 'Our people have been waiting for you for thousands of years.' He sought Gurudev's help in preserving their traditions and value systems. Having met the people there and organized a meditation programme, Gurudev wanted to leave immediately, but the locals insisted that he stay a little longer. Finally, when it was time to leave, a blizzard started and, as a result, they were forced to extend their stay by a day. The group was not prepared for this and had no food or other provisions with them. The plan was to leave the next day, but when they took to the skies again, they got caught engulfed in a snowstorm. The pilot could see absolutely nothing and warned the group that they could crash any moment. But Gurudev instructed the group to chant

'*Om Namah Shivaya*,' which had a calming effect on them, in sharp contrast to the blazing fury outside. One can either have a master or be hounded by the mind's cravings, aversions and fears. The tranquility rubbed off on the pilot, too, who surrendered completely to what the moment had to offer. Not long after, a hole appeared in the storm below and the pilot immediately dived in. Wondrously, the hole had appeared above the runway of the airport and they managed to land.

The airport authorities interrogated the pilot for landing without permission, but he managed to explain to them that they were left with no other choice! Marcy, who was on the flight, told me that while the absurd argument about the unauthorized landing was going on, Gurudev stepped out of the plane. A member of the maintenance staff was startled to see him, probably because of the long hair and beard and the white robes, and exclaimed, 'Jesus!' Soon enough, the discussions came to an end, and they were escorted to safety. While narrating this incident, Gurudev told us that there was a time when he was contemplating on whether to continue with his life or not. He had already established institutions that could spread the knowledge but he could also see the faces of people who were still waiting for him. He had told us that there are phases in one's life when one can choose to leave the body, just like exiting a freeway. There are unseen forces governing this creation and they have a role to play in these moments. He says, 'Lift your eyes and see—the world of the gods is just inches above you!' What we see as the manifest universe is but the tip of an iceberg. Whereas science tries to unravel the mysteries of what is perceivable, spirituality deepens our understanding of creation around us and takes us into the realms of the unknown. To walk this pathless path, a guru's guidance is essential.

Gurudev says that when one is about to leave one's body, only two important questions remain. 'How much love has one given? How much wisdom has one gained?' By training us to become teachers of meditation, he brought about a paradigm shift in our lives. Knowledge can be imparted only with love, which turns it into profound wisdom. I have met prisoners who have experienced a higher quality of life thanks to the wisdom from Art of Living's prison programmes. Similarly, distresseded farmers saw a new ray of hope, and exasperated students, who felt they had disappointed their parents, saw the troubled relationship in a new light and had their self-confidence restored. Fishermen who had lost everything during the tsunami could venture into the waters again after practising breathing techniques, and children in Gaza who struggled to close their eyes because of nightmares could now sleep peacefully. Several previously radicalized Kashmiri men are now working to relieve the trauma of others after being exposed to the programme. Young men and women who thought that their success owes to their achievements now recognize that the sign of real success is nothing but an undying smile. People from every sphere of life—irrespective of language, faith, age, profession, education—have experienced this transformation and have felt a fountain of joy springing from within them. Every time I experience something similar, I feel that teaching is the art of caring. People come to Gurudev with fruits, sweets and flowers as gifts, and he tells them, 'Blossom in your smile! That is the real gift for me.'

Gurudev was in Paris for his thirty-third birthday and

many had brought gifts for him. He would receive a neatly wrapped gift package from one person and would give it to another person, and this continued. He often says, 'If you really want to give me a gift, spread the wisdom '. Once, a small boy came to him for blessings on his birthday. Gurudev gave him some sweets and told him to share it with people. The boy shared the sweets and came back for more. Gurudev gave him more sweets, and the process continued. This happened several times when the volunteers on stage looked at Gurudev not knowing what to do. He told them, 'Let him come. As long as he keeps sharing, I will keep giving.'

There are many people, young and old, who come to him and experience a spark being kindled inside. They see the purpose and meaning of being an Art of Living teacher. Harish Ramachandran, one such young teacher, shared with me what Gurudev told a gathering of several hundred people, 'Each and every cell of my body is here for you.' A change in consciousness from a space of want and need to being always there for people happens in the teacher's training programme. Gaspar Insfran, a young boy from Paraguay who was addicted to drugs, was relieved of his addiction after experiencing Sudarshan Kriya. He now teaches the course to similarly affected youth, helping them come out of their misery. A young girl from Mumbai brought warring factions together in Ivory Coast, another from Gujarat got militants to lay down their arms in Manipur, a member of a royal family in Kerala worked to mitigate the trauma of thousands in Sri Lanka, a girl from Himachal Pradesh taught yoga to people from hundreds of nationalities—ordinary people leading extraordinary lives as they spread the light of wisdom within them.

When one wears a diamond, one's stride changes as the precious stone brings confidence and dignity to one's bearing. Gurudev says, 'Walk like a king, and be a perfect servant. You are part of the divine and carry precious wisdom within you. Even as you feel like a king inwardly, you should be a servant to the people outwardly. Only then can you be of service to humanity.' Every Art of Living teacher has been given the golden opportunity to sow this seed of wisdom, to bring happiness and joy to everyone around them.

Once, during the day of Guru Purnima, Gurudev said, 'The giver provides for us tirelessly. But not only does he not want any recognition from us, he also makes us feel as if it is our own achievement. The infinity keeps giving in abundance. We have to put it to good use, not for one's own benefit, but for the benefit of society. Serving the world is akin to paying obeisance to the divine. When we honour the wisdom that we have received by sharing it, our life is elevated.'

This incident happened when I had gone to the US with Gurudev for the first time. He was on stage and I was seated in the front row. He gestured towards me to come on stage. When I went up, he asked me to sing before promptly closing his eyes. I had never sung in public before and looked at him, but his eyes were still closed. So I closed mine, too, and sang a Ganesha stuti. Gurudev said, 'When a little bird sings, it is the voice of the infinity that flows through it'. I felt the same as the music flowed through me. I once again looked at him, and he opened his eyes and smiled. Ever since, I have never had any hesitation to be on stage or to sing.

There is a couplet by saint Kabir, which says that when he cried out in search of Rama everywhere, he could not find him. But when he said, where am 'I'? There is no me without you—he found Rama everywhere. Gurudev says that his teachers are part of his soul. Gurudev is such a good friend to me, accepting me as I am and guiding me on things that require improvement. Wherever I direct my feelings and emotions, he is there. Dedicating songs of love to the Master feels just right as the Guru is a mirror to me. Whatever one is, he reflects it. That is why one feels comforted and contented. There is no difference of opinion or arguments. Even as a brother, he has never bossed over me, but he is my biggest and only boss! The effect of having a guru is so subtle that it is impossible to separate one's identity from that of one's guru.

Once, one of our teachers shared with Gurudev that everyone in the satsang appreciated his talk and wisdom. Gurudev asked him, 'Your talk? Your wisdom?' He got the message immediately. He was forgetting that he is an instrument in the hands of the divine. Two days later, an article featuring me came in the newspaper entitled, 'In the Shadow of her Brother.' The journalist who had interviewed me captured whatever I had wanted to share very well. This was over twenty years ago and it was a big thing to have such a feature appear in the papers. Swami Sadyojatah showed it to Gurudev and praised the article. The memory of what Gurudev said to the teacher was fresh in my mind. So I interjected and said, "Gurudev, it's all you!" He instantly looked at me and said, 'Take ownership. Where did "you" come from? Be in advait (oneness)!' I was taken aback. Two similar situations had elicited totally opposite responses from him. You simply cannot predict what he is going to say next! Gurudev's words describing the guru come to my mind here. He says, 'If you are dull, he is brilliant. If you are brilliant, he is irrational. If you are irrational, he is irresistible. If you are complaining, he is tough. If you are perfect, he is imperfection personified!' Laughingly he adds, 'Having a guru is inviting all sorts of trouble! Do you really want to have one?'

12

LOVE IS NOT AN EMOTION

My heart rises in waves and
Lashes at your feet, for
Eternity, oh dear!
This creation is nothing
But a celebration
Of thy presence.

I see you in the leaves and
In the petals
And in the stems, in the thorns,
And in the Unseen Roots
It's all you, and you, and you
Nothing but you.

Whether in the bark or the thorns
Or the Roots in the Mud

Your face is Reflected
Smiling and
Dancing and
Laughing and
Singing

It's all you
It's all you.

In tears of joy
In tears of sorrow alike
You play, you dance, you sing
And you celebrate.
It's all you
It's all you
It's all you
For each glorifies the other.

Everything in this Creation
Glorifies everything else.
Clapping your own hands together
You Rejoice in My Presence
It's all you
It's all you
It's all you.

THERE IS AN island in the Atlantic Ocean from where mountains on the mainland are visible. The shores of the island are rocky with untamed waves crashing on it day and night. The wind blows with abandon on the island's pristine expanse. Gurudev stood silently on the shore as waves encircled his feet, spraying him with mists of cool water. He was facing the ocean and the mountains on the mainland. He was still, but his robes, long hair and beard danced to the breeze. This beautiful image was captured in a photograph that I still keep with me.

In the summer of 1990, Gurudev visited a scenic island in Nova Scotia, Canada, called Cape Breton. Kishan and

Bharti Verma, a couple who are volunteers from Canada, were driving him there. They crossed a bridge en route when Gurudev suddenly exclaimed, 'Oh! So this bridge is here?' It was not a bridge of any special significance and not many wayfarers used it. 'I have seen the faces of people who are waiting beyond this bridge.' It was not immediately obvious to us if he was referring to the actual people who lived beyond the bridge or if he was considering it as a milestone at that point in time. No one asked. They reached Cape Breton soon after, and Gurudev said he could perceive Narada Bhakti sutras (aphorisms of love) echoing from the mountains in the area. Soon after, he started giving talks on the sutras. They translated into experience even as we heard the Master speak. The talks happened over a period of three months as Gurudev toured various cities across Canada and the US. Some talks were given as part of advanced courses, and others were delivered as public talks. As every talk began with the rather abrupt 'And the next sutra is ...' statement, newcomers would be confused in the beginning. 'So what happened before this?' people would ask. But by the time he would get into his talk, all confusion would vanish and their minds would be back to the present. Sometimes, Gurudev would intersperse his talks with spontaneously composed love poems.

During a short period of the tour, Gurudev stayed in a Zen monastery and remarked during a talk that the air was filled with Zen koans. He once started off by saying, 'And the next sutra is $2+1=0$,' and for the rest of the evening we were trying to figure what that meant! At another venue, he came in, sat down, and started meditating. After about forty minutes or so, he opened his eyes and said, '... and that was the next sutra' and walked off!

One of our stops during the tour was at the Loon Lake in Cape Breton, where his commentary on the ancient Bhakti sutras was characterized by unusual depths of love and devotion. Gurudev stayed at a cabin, which was completely made of wood, including the chandeliers. 'This is just how the divine is! The entire creation is made up of that one divinity, just as everything in this room is made of wood.' This was his answer to the aphoristic sutra '2+1= 0'. Years later, he recounted this incident to a few spiritual leaders from the Swami Narayan tradition. The world is full of opposites: joy and sorrow, the high and the low. Once we perceive and realize the divine, this duality ceases to exist.

An advanced course was organized at the venue, too, which culminated in Guru Purnima celebrations. On the very first night of our stay, we were woken up in the middle of the night and requested to reach the course venue. I changed quickly with childlike excitement! We were getting bonus time with the Master and slumber took an instant back seat. I am not so sure if sleep was so kind to others as well as some participants looked half-asleep as they ambled along in the direction of the main hall. As we entered the hall, we saw Gurudev, who looked like the bright morning sun in the middle of that special night. 'Mosquitoes were singing to us, so I thought of singing to them too.' And we had the most magical satsang under the night sky.

During our stay, a skit was prepared by some of the participants. Barry Parnell, a television scriptwriter, was part of the meditation course. With his help, a script for an episode along the lines of the sitcom 'I Love Lucy', entitled 'When Lucy met her Guru', was drafted. Philip Fraser donned the role of Gurudev—his long hair was just perfect for the role. Robin Vance was Lucy Ricardo, greeting Gurudev and giving him gifts. She tripped and made a faux pas, which meant not much acting was required! John Osborne was Fred Mertz, Sudarshana Penner was Ethel Mertz, and Michael Fischman enacted Ricky Ricardo. They played the skit in front of Gurudev, and to our delight, he was in splits throughout!

With each passing day, the moon over the lake was waxing, and so were our hearts. The full moon looks twice as big, if not more, in this part of the world compared with Indian skies. It felt a lot nearer too. It was as if the moon wanted to be closer to the Master as well. Many such moons have passed, but our hearts remain full and content. Often we get angry over minor things, such as a misplaced shoe or a missing cherry on a cake. The mind remains disturbed, even after the cake is long gone. A guru can turn around this pattern completely, and one's mind remains calm and positive, undisturbed by the small nothings of life.

For our guru puja, we arranged flowers, fruits, incense sticks, sandalwood paste and water—an expression of our gratitude for masters who have kept the wisdom going for so many years. The roses were in full bloom on the table, a white handkerchief was neatly folded and placed on a coconut, and a tealight candle waited for the arrival of the Master. The log cabin was decorated with balloons and streamers as if it was a birthday party. Wisdom assumed a childlike innocence that expressed itself in colourful decorations. We sat on the carpet in front of Gurudev's chair, waiting with unhurried eagerness. Our lilting melodies merged into one another and with the music around us. When it dawned upon us that the Master was about to arrive, the tempo of our song rose. Gurudev lit the candle and incense sticks. He delicately held a rose between his fingers and started chanting in his soft voice. Our eyes closed as we were transported to an ethereal space, where we stayed in meditation for a long time. We sat in silence for a few minutes once we opened our eyes.

When he finally spoke, the sweetness of his words was indescribable. He told us about the three types of people who come to a master—students, disciples and devotees.

A student goes to a teacher to learn something. All of you went to primary schools, middle schools and secondary schools and learned about computers, about mathematics. A student collects information, but information is not knowledge, not wisdom. Information cannot produce change. A disciple comes to the master for the sake of wisdom, for improving his life, and for attaining enlightenment. He has a purpose, so he is not just collecting information but is trying to look a little deeper to bring a transformation in his life. A disciple, however, is still centred on his self and as per his capacity may grow and get enlightened one day. And then there is the devotee, who comes to the master not even for wisdom. He is simply rejoicing in love. He has fallen in deep love with the master, the infinity, with god. He doesn't care whether he is enlightened or not. For a devotee, being immersed in divine love is enough. We can see students everywhere, but disciples are fewer in number and devotees rare.

It is beautiful to shed tears of love. Those who have cried in love even once know the taste of surrender and devotion. The entire being longs for just one thing—tears of bitterness transforming into tears of sweetness, of love. Gurudev said that Guru Purnima is the day of the devotee. He spoke of Sariputra, a disciple of Buddha, who only wanted to serve his master, yet Buddha asked him to spread wisdom as he had attained enlightenment. Gurudev also spoke of the love that gopikas and gopis had towards Lord Krishna. While speaking, his eyes welled up with tears of love. Most participants were wiping their eyes as a sense of gratitude filled the entire room. Singing 'Radhe Govind', Gurudev went into a trance, holding a beautiful mudra. All of us, about a hundred people, stood around him, singing. We were all on a journey to eternity and our consciousness was expanding in no time to touch infinity.

After the satsang, Gurudev went on a raft ride on the lake. Everybody wanted to be on the same raft with him. So he ended up making many trips up and down the lake. He was pulling the rope that helped navigate the raft. Suzannah, Philip, Kishan Verma—there were many flautists who took turns playing melodies that reverberated back from the mountains and filled the space around us. The water splashing against the raft, the far-off ethereal echoes of solitary loons calling to each other, the coolness of the moonlight, eyes shining in the dark, the presence of a master, I could not help but sing an old Kannada song, 'Ambiga Naa Ninna Nambidhe ...' which means, 'O Lord, you are my boatman, I depend on you to carry me across to the other shore ...' As the song ended, he said, 'It is beautiful, so beautiful. That is why we have to come back again and again.'

I don't know why this happens
When I look at you, my heart bursts open
And flows in love

Thrills my creation
I don't know why this happens to me.

Like the Firecracker that rises far up in the dark sky
And fills it with showers of light
I don't know why this happens to me

I don't know why this happens to me
As Breath flows through me
To the dance of the fingers
And you hear the melody
I don't know why this happens to me.

Everything passes, and the last day of the course was upon us. Many were quite sad at the prospect of having to leave. Everyone wanted to follow Gurudev as far as they could. We were all sad, seated around him in a log cabin. He smiled and requested us to turn around and face the opposite wall. We protested, wanting to face him. He said, 'Please know that I am always behind you', and asked us to meditate. 'Can you still feel my presence? It will be the same once I leave. I will still be with you.' In those moments, we perceived the presence of a master beyond anything tangible, a master who is always with us, at every moment of our lives.

After the Guru Purnima celebrations at the lake, the group followed Gurudev to other parts of Halifax to immerse themselves in the continuing talks on Bhakti Sutras and participate in more advanced meditation programmes. One of the new venues was a school basketball court converted into a meditation hall with a stage. One of those days, Gurudev asked Bharti Verma to prepare colours for playing Holi (although it was not really the day of Holi). With buckets of water, sandalwood paste and flowers, we had so much fun splashing colours at each other. Yet another day, on Gurudev's instructions, Philip and a few others replaced the belongings of each participant with another's. After a stint of deep meditation, we streamed into our rooms in silence only to be in chaos again! It was an interesting experience to see how attached we were to our small possessions and how the mind that was in such deep calmness fell back to total turbulence in a matter of seconds. Everyone got their luggage back, but a lucky few also learned about the nature of the human mind itself.

On the next full-moon day after Guru Purnima, as we were singing 'Sri Radhe Radhe Radhe Shyam ...' at our satsang, Gurudev started walking out of the hall. We followed him. Philip was asked to get his flute along. Gurudev walked into a clearing, and we spread out to form a circle as we continued to sing. Sometimes he would come inside the circle, sometimes he would go out of it. Our hearts danced along with each of his steps. Each time he turned around, our entire being felt the swirl as we watched him. The skies, the stars, the moon, the grass, the trees, the gentle breeze—nature seemed to be celebrating along with us. We were witnessing something that was not of this world, something that was eternal.

'You are a piece of music yourself, an unsung song. You are the song of silence. To get to that depth, it is good to sing, and if you feel like dancing dance too. Involve yourself fully with your mind and body. That becomes ecstasy,' said Gurudev later in the evening. Recollecting these precious moments, Suzannah said, 'We had all fallen in love with the exquisite, funny, adorable and totally unattainable form of the guru. On the one hand, he was childlike and playful; on the other, he was as ancient and deep as the universe. But beyond falling in love with the form of the guru, we had indeed fallen in love with infinity!' Gurudev often says, 'Love is not an emotion. It is your very existence.'

13

SINK AND BE SAVED!

WE WERE RIDING out a storm on a boat en route to the Maldives. It looked as if ours was the only boat on the waters that day. Gurudev had been invited to the residence of the president of the Maldives for dinner. The tumultuous waves rose several feet high and tossed the boat. The sound of the crashing waves could only be matched by the heavy drumbeat of the downpour. It looked as if we had signed up for an adventure.

The captain of the vessel was a confident and skilled man. He looked all set to take on the fury of the sea, and intensely focused on predicting the next wave so he could manoeuvre us to safety. At one point, a wave rose like a giant wall of water in front of us, and we looked like tiny specks in front of its enormity. There was no way we were going to escape it. What was the captain going to do now? He somehow turned the boat in a direction perpendicular to the wave even as it was rising above us. We forged across and were soon racing through a tunnel of water for what seemed like eternity before the captain managed to successfully break through it as the wave crashed behind us. My mind experienced each moment of this phenomenon with a sense of total awe and not fear. The same mind has witnessed several other storms—of emotions—rising and ebbing over the past many years. Wisdom is the only way to ride these storms. If we let ourselves sink in wisdom, we will be saved from drowning in our own emotions.

Having arrived at the president's residence, we were served tea. The stability of the land was greatly comforting after the tumultuous journey. As I picked up the dainty teacup, tiny ripples formed on the tea infused with delicate flavours. These waves were gentle, similar to the waves of bliss that one experiences in the presence of a master. When the Master speaks, it translates into experience. His discourses lead us to a journey of self-discovery.

One such discourse took place in August 1991 in the Bangalore ashram. Sincere seekers with a deep thirst for knowledge had gathered from around the world. Gurudev had told each one of them, 'Come to the ashram in August.' So they came. But no one knew what was in store for them. During the evening satsang, he walked into the Devi Hall in what seemed to be the deepest silence. Just seeing him walk stirred something deep within me. From that space of intense silence, he spoke on the Ashtavakra Gita, which is written in the form of a dialogue between Sage Ashtavakra and Janaka, the king of Mithila. Throughout the discourse, my heart was content like that of a sage even as my intellect sought more, like a progressive king. It was a thirty-three day programme, and before each talk, Gurudev would lead us to sing the song 'Alakh Niranjana'—the untouched etheral one. I felt transported into another world in those moments of singing. His commentary on the Ashtavakra Gita turned one's life, thinking and world upside down. Concepts were broken, patterns changed, new horizons of understanding achieved. At the end of each talk, he would announce birthdays and anniversaries of the participants, and it would feel as if we were switching to another reality, with a mundane back-to-earth feeling. But he lived across both the realities. The birthday cake was cut with as much attention as the concepts in our mind.

I was fortunate to be present at the talk and participate in two other programmes where the talks were being given in other languages. 'Who is God?', 'Storms of emotions', 'Rejoicing without conflict', 'Types of space'—these were some of the titles of those lectures. Even now, when I listen to their recorded versions, I feel new doors and new dimensions opening up to me. Soon after, Gurudev gave a commentary on the Yoga Sutras of Patanjali at Weggis, Switzerland. One gets to learn about the human body, the structure of a leaf or other such tangible things in detail but seldom about the mind, which has always been treated as a subtle unknown dimension that psychologists are still struggling to grasp. But in the Yoga Sutras, the sage has expounded on the nature of our mind with great clarity and detail. A fish cannot grasp an ocean's totality, but a bird's eye view will surely give us a sense of its vastness. Only one who is anchored in the self can speak about the mind with clarity.

During one of his tours to the west coast of the US, Gurudev gave a number of talks which were simply called the 'Santa Monica Series'. After he gave a talk on Jesus Christ, a gentleman asked Gurudev about his take on Mary Magdalene. Although he said he had not read much about her, he closed his eyes for a few minutes and delivered a talk on her. The gentleman thanked him and said that Gurudev's commentary was indeed in line with the current thinking about Mary Magdalene.

One of those days, when he was scheduled to speak at an event in Santa Monica, there was a power outage, which affected large parts of the city. Some volunteers who lived about ten minutes away found that it would take at least an hour and a half for them to reach the venue. They called up to enquire about the event and asked if it should be postponed. Gurudev assured them that power would come back in time for the talk, and it did. Thousands came to the Santa Monica Civic Auditorium to hear the Master talk, experience his profound silence in guided meditations, and sing, dance and celebrate along with him. Gurudev's talks were entitled 'The ancient new age', 'The cosmic connection: planets, stars and life', 'The ultimate relationship', 'Jesus: The embodiment of love', 'Buddha: The manifestation of silence', 'Krishna: Absolute joy', and 'Death and beyond'. The talks were made available on tape immediately, so that people could carry them back home. I was left with the realization that the love of Jesus, the silence of Buddha and the joy of Krishna were now available to me in my life's path. During the talks, one participant asked Gurudev about 'used cars'. Until then, I was of the opinion that if one asks questions to a spiritual master, they should be about love, god, or similar topics. I thought it was disrespectful to even broach topics outside of this ambit. Although the man was trying to be funny, Gurudev spent a good forty minutes imparting upon us the deepest wisdom illustrated through the idea of used cars in the most humorous way! He compared recharging batteries to rejuvenating and refreshing the mind and so on and showed us how humour was an essential component of practical wisdom. He surprised us all by finding valuable wisdom even in the most mundane things.

Once Gurudev was invited to inaugurate a Shiva temple and satsang hall at the Sri Adichunchanagiri Mutt Blind School. One-hundred-and-twenty-five teacher trainees accompanied Gurudev to the inaugural venue and then to the nearby scenic waterfalls. It was an exquisite evening. Nature was at her best with golden-hued skies, exquisite cloud patterns, rolling hills, pleasant weather and magnificent waterfalls. Dinesh Ghodke, a young teacher from the Indian Institute of Technology, suddenly exclaimed, 'We should have come here without Gurudev!' Everybody around was startled as they had come to the falls because of Gurudev. But Dinesh immediately added, 'Now we are only looking at Gurudev!' Gurudev smiled and replied, 'Look at the waterfall. If a rock falls, it breaks into pieces, but when water falls it generates power and is beautiful to look at. Being somebody is like being a rock, being nobody is like being water, and being everybody is like being water vapour.'

Spirituality has always been seen as something abstract and unknowable. But the simplicity of Gurudev's profound wisdom has made it easy for so many people to easily connect with the spiritual path. He says our enthusiasm should be like that of a candle flame that rises upward even if the candle were to be held upside down. At the same time, water flows downward, no matter whatever height at which it is stored, teaching us humility. The water droplet on the lotus leaf reminds us of dispassion. The coconut tree, its fruits, leaves and stem, used for different things, teaches us to be useful to others in every possible way. The life cycle of a butterfly reminds us of the transformation that we undergo when we come to a master. The entire beehive disappears when the queen bee goes away—the queen bee is similar to the divine within us. The flower reminds us of a completely blossomed consciousness. The hollow bamboo flute teaches us to be a perfect instrument in the hands of the divine. Thus, every creation around us has a message that helps us to be in touch with our deeper self.

One day, a family friend brought a fax machine, the latest gadget of that time, to Manjula, our home in Bangalore. This invention was magical—what one wrote in one part of the world could be printed in another! Soon after, Gurudev travelled to the US, and at Big Sur, California, the very first knowledge sheet was born. Every Wednesday evening, he would ask those around him for a choice of topics. He would then speak around those topics, which would be typed out and faxed to Art of Living centres around the world to be read out during satsangs on Thursdays. My mother would eagerly wait near the fax machine every Thursday and would not let anyone see the fax sheet until she was done reading it. She was not really proficient in English but still wanted to read it all by herself. I would wait for my turn impatiently—the knowledge would always be brisk, crisp, sweet and punchy.

Once, during Navaratri, Gurudev had entered into a deep meditative silence. Swami Sadyojatah made Gurudev's bed, locked his bedroom, and left for the day. He had forgotten to ask for the weekly knowledge sheet before Gurudev went into his silence. A little later he realized what had happened, and while mulling over what to do next, a few boys at the ashram came running to him with a piece of paper with something written on it. They said that Gurudev had handed it over to them. But that was not possible as Swamiji had locked Gurudev in and he had entered into silence. Yet the knowledge sheet was in his hand and no one else could have spoken those words!

Prayer within breath
Is silence
Breath within love
Is silence
Love within infinity
Is silence
Wisdom without words
Is silence
Compassion without aim
Is silence
Action without doer
Is silence
Smiling with all of existence
Is silence!

The knowledge sheets would connect us to Gurudev wherever he was. The sheets, which Gurudev called 'Intimate notes to the sincere seeker', were a continuous commitment for seven years. When the series ended, there were 365 knowledge sheets—one for each day of the year.

The first time Gurudev travelled to Poland for an advanced course in 1990, Scott Hague, an Art of Living teacher from the US, was travelling with him. He would later share his experience with me. Although it was late when they arrived, the course participants were eagerly waiting for Gurudev. The Polish group had a tradition of handing out candles at night, passing one flame after another until the entire room would glow like a Christmas evening. Gurudev sat in the room silent and graceful, and soon after, they retired to bed. The next morning, Gurudev talked about why it was unnecessary to react if someone were to blow up in anger. At that very moment, a power surge blew out the bulb of an expensive camera recorder. Not missing a beat, Gurudev said, 'See when things explode around you, make sure that you keep your smile going.' On the last day, everyone was brought out of their silence. As they started sharing their experiences, the participants talked about the wonderful transformations they had undergone and asked Gurudev what they could do in return. He replied:

Service is an expression of love. Serve in whatever possible ways you can. A tree is so useful. It gives oxygen, shade and wood for furniture and fuel. Even when a tree is dead, it continues to be useful. Similarly, we should ask how we could be useful to people around us and the whole world. Then our hearts start blossoming and a completely new life begins. Otherwise, we would always be engulfed in ourselves, worried only about our well-being, which is such a waste of time! In another fifty years, we may not be here, but while we are around, let's do the best we can. And the best gift is the gift of knowledge. One may give this or that, but nothing lasts as long as the knowledge of uplifting one's mind. Happiness is about knowing the eternal nature of life and a true gift is nothing but sharing this knowledge with everybody around us.

14

THE GRAND PLAY OF PLAYS

THE MAROON COLOURED, nine-yard silk sari felt soft and sacred in my hands as I carefully took it out of my wardrobe. Navaratri was around the corner—the nine nights of the festival representing the nine months that a baby spends in its mother's womb. My mother used to be draped in silk all of those nine days. I was more interested in the regular six-yard saris as they were more elaborately and uniquely designed, while the nine-yard silks were usually plain. I got matching bangles and bindis and selected the saris to wear on each day, but the main focus was on preparing myself. Whenever my mother asked me to wear the nine-yard silks, I evaded her. 'You wear it, it is too long for me,' I would say.

I sat with her for the puja, enjoying the chants, the meditation and the colours. At home, papier-mâché dolls used to be arranged on structures that were made for the occasion. When we were little, Gurudev and I would go from one house to another to see those dolls. I would dress up in a silk skirt and blouse with my braided hair adorned with jasmine flowers. In each house, we would be asked to sing a song, which we dutifully did with a few practised lines. Once we were done with the song, we were given shundal, savouries made of lentils. We would carry the 'bounty' back home, and our mother would inspect it and let us eat whatever was found okay. As we grew up, chanting the 'Lalitha Sahasranama' used to be part of the routine all through the nine days of Navaratri until one day Gurudev decided to perform the Chandi yagya, which is undertaken for the benefit of all.

A yagya honours the divine in its various manifestations and purifies the body, mind and environment. It works on our collective consciousness and uplifts us all. Navaratri had always been a celebratory festival; now the dimension of meditative chants and silence were added to it. Gurudev used to go into deep silence on such days, which had a strong impact on me too. Thoughts would be hard to come by during these periods, and I would have to plan everything beforehand. The chants would take me to another realm altogether. This continued for several years until I had to take charge of the festivities myself. Amma passed away in 1999, and I had to wear the nine-yard sari for the first time. It was not easy for me as wearing the sari was a long process that required the help of experienced elders, and each time, it felt like an ordeal for me. On top of it, my husband would hurry me saying, 'Wear your sari soon or we will miss the muhurtham (the auspicious period of time).'

The yagyas begin on the sixth day of Navaratri. The afternoon of the fifth day was dedicated to wearing mehendi in elaborate floral patterns. All the girls would participate in this ceremony, which was a beautiful art form in itself. The next day, Anna woke me up at 4 a.m. It was too early for any activity other than meditation. Perhaps I was a little lazy too. But Anna explained that we needed to leave early from Manjula to avoid traffic. So I got up and got ready, but when we reached the old meditation hall at the ashram where the yagyas were to be performed, there was hardly anybody there. Even the pundits had not come so early! In the early morning silence, everything looked fresh with the flower arrangements especially looking delicate and colourful. The hall was cleaned with cow dung in the traditional way.

That particular day, three new homa kundas (sacred pits for sacrificial fires) were arranged in the hall. The pundits trickled in and started making geometrical patterns on the floor with rice flour, turmeric and a few other natural colours. Their fingers moved deftly to make perfectly symmetrical patterns. Later on, Gurudev told me that those drawings were yantras—diagrams that facilitate the movement of energies and denote various aspects of our mind and body. That a hand-drawn diagram could be a channel for the movement of energies was intriguing! The hall filled up quickly and the pujas were about to begin. Gurudev also came. I went in with Anna, bowed down to Gurudev, and took my seat. At that moment, I suddenly felt grown up and mature. I felt like my mother.

The chants began, and as I looked around, everything started coming to life. Whatever I had seen before, I now perceived with a mature pair of eyes. When I saw the attendees, I thought, 'Are they comfortable? Do they need anything?' Bangles and saris were not high priority any more. When I was young, I used to dream of a house with many girls, boys, women, and men—the women would cook many different dishes, chat and sing with great a sense of togetherness. As I looked around the hall, I realized that my dream had come

Gurudev performing aarti during
Rudra Puja at the Bangalore ashram

Pitaji sprinkling holy water
from a puja on Gurudev during
Navaratri in the late 1990s

Gurudev playing the veena
during the Navaratri pujas

Gurudev giving darshan
during the Navaratri pujas

Gurudev on the banks of the Ganga
in Rishikesh with Pragyanandji
Maharaj and other saints

Gurudev meditating
by the water in the La
Maurice National Park in
the Laurentian Mountains,
Quebec, Canada

Gurudev wearing the Sikh traditional attire during a tour through Punjab

Gurudev listening to the concerns of Bengali Muslims during the violence that broke out between them and the indigenous Bodo groups in Assam, 2012

Gurudev meeting and distributing sweets to Yezidi children in refugee camps in the Sinjar Mountains, Iraq, 2014

Gurudev addressing a peace conference entitled 'Protecting Women and Bringing Stability and Peace' in the Kurdish capital of Erbil, 2014

Gurudev in discussion with the
speaker of the Kurdish parliament,
Dr Yusuf Mohammed, 2014

Gurudev with FARC (Revolutionary
Armed Forces of Colombia—
People's Army) leaders Ivan Marquez
and Paulo Catatumbo at a press
conference in Havana, 2015

Gurudev after receiving an honorary doctorate from the Nyenrode University, Netherlands, 2012

Gurudev receiving the highest civilian award from the Government of Colombia, 2016

Gurudev aṣ the keynote speaker in an interfaith conference hosted by the World Bank and the Turkish Ethical Values Centre Foundation in Turkey, 2004

Gurudev addressing the participants of the World Forum for Ethics in Business at the European Parliament, Brussels

Gurudev in a public event
in Argentina, 2012

Gurudev at a public event,
'The Planet Meditates', in Buenos
Aires where 150,000 Argentinians
had gathered, 2012

The view from the stage during the Silver Jubilee Celebrations, 2006

Gurudev at a
Mahasatsang in Kerala

Pitaji greeting the former
president of India, H.E.
Dr A.P.J Abdul Kalam,
during the Silver Jubilee
Celebrations, Bangalore,
February 2006

A view of the stage during the World Cultural Festival where over 3.5 million people had gathered on the banks of River Yamuna, New Delhi, 2016

Gurudev at the event entitled 'Meri Dilli Meri Yamuna' in New Delhi to inspire people to volunteer to clean up the Yamuna River in March 2010

Gurudev along with hundreds of
volunteers in several boats removing
tonnes of garbage from the river,
2010

true: everyone was dressed up in their best attire and wore a joyous smile with a palpable longing for the divine. I sat there with these musings in my mind, which were harmonious like music and comforting. The bhajans at the event were melodious, even ethereal. The whole gathering was in a trance. When the final ahuti (grand offering at the culmination of a yagya) happened, I experienced the presence of Ganesha in Gurudev himself. I was sitting in front of him but felt as if I were in front of an enormous elephant. I have seen the Ganesha idol at Lal Bagh, which is so majestic that you would feel tiny in front of it. I felt the same in front of Gurudev at that moment. His presence was powerful, yet gentle. Within a few minutes, the yagya was over, and it was time for lunch.

The evening was dedicated to Chandi prarambha—the beginning of the Chandi homa. India is a land of rishis (sages) and krishis (farmers). Every puja starts with a beeja vaapana—nine types of seeds are sown in small clay pots and a mixture of milk and water is sprayed on them. Gurudev says that life and puja are no different. Life itself is a puja. When we walk, it is pradakshina (circumambulation); when we eat, it is naivedyam (offering of food) and so on. This attitude brings purity in life. When there is purity, the mind is strong, the intellect is sharp, and there is enthusiasm. Even to sow a seed, an auspicious time is chosen. A group of seven women, attired in nine yards, smiling, and checking if their legs were covered properly, sowed the seeds with devotion. Nobody could possibly decipher how they actually felt, but there was gaiety and laughter, and a sense of deep happiness.

The next morning was the time for Rudra homa. Rudra is an aspect of Lord Shiva. As the homas progressed, the presence of divine energy became more and more discernible. That evening Gurudev played the veena, my younger son Arvind played the tabla, Manikantan Menon played the flute, and little Malvika played the sitar. Time just flew by. The music and the sequence of songs had been planned and rehearsed over many days, but when it started, it was all over in just a few moments.

The most awaited Maha chandi homa was conducted the next morning. There was excitement in the early morning air with the fluttering dragonflies, the cooing cuckoos, and the joyous anticipation of the Mother Divine. There were nine women, the sumangalis, in their nine-yard saris; the dhampati, the elderly couple; the nine kanyas, all dressed up like young devis; the vatus, the brahmin boys; the pundits; the 108 types of herbs that were offered to agni; the yantra diagrams; the fragrance; Indrani and Maheshwara, the elephants of the ashram; and the rhythmic chants—everything came together in harmony.

When I look back, every detail is magnified. The pictures look like perfect portraits. Everybody looks beautiful and happy. In that field of serenity, the Devi, invoked in a kalash (pot of water), rose with all her paraphernalia with the drums beating and conches blowing. Flowers were showered accompanied by Vedic chants, and she was carried on the head of the chief priest with their path guided by Gurudev. Devotees stood along the path with folded arms soaking in the magnificence of the Devi. I accompanied her, overwhelmed by her loving and powerful presence, thinking 'I have to wait for a whole year to experience her like this again!' But then I consoled myself that she would be always in my heart.

The sacred water in the pot is offered to Gurudev and then sprinkled on the devotees. It was a kind of divine play, a leela, within the schema of that larger leela called life. Yet it was a very grand play. Each year I would feel the same, 'This is it! This is the life that is worth living for!' One may not understand the incantations or many of the proceedings that constitute the puja, but that hardly matters. The inquisitive intellect has no place where one is in the depth of one's own being.

The next day dawned with the Rishi homa—honouring Vedic sages who have kept the tradition alive. Each day transitioned to another as gracefully as one yoga posture would progress to another. Gurudev performed the Guru puja on this day. As I started chanting the mantras, my students from all over the world joined me. I felt like a mother hen proud of her chicks! That was the sattvic ego in action, but I did not mind having it. As each day's puja concluded, we sang '*Abhayam, abhayam amma ...*', a song dedicated to the Divine Mother, seeking her shelter. My mother always sang this song as part of her puja; Gurudev would go into a trance listening to this song with his hands forming graceful mudras. The energy and beauty in his movements are indescribable. During those moments, I approach him with an arti plate and circumambulate him. The sacredness of that moment is unparalleled for me. Everything is illumined and effulgent. Faces dissolve and I see everyone around me as just light. One day, two professionals specializing in Kirlian photography came to the ashram and took pictures of the hall and pujas during a Rishi homa. When the photographs were processed, they could see the movement of varying energies, in multiple colours, across the hall. There was an enormous field of green light emanating from Gurudev, which extended even beyond the hall. They said green was the colour of healing. Almost every individual meditating in the hall had a vibrant aura around them. I felt that my experience has been authenticated.

The ashram members had installed sprinklers on the ceiling of the yagyashala, which would sprinkle holy water from the Ganga and other rivers. At the culmination of the homa, the sprinkle would fall like a shower of blessings on everyone. I felt as if I were immersing myself in the holy Ganga and remembered my mother. I was grateful to her for preparing me for this experience. During the last puja in which she was present, she said that she felt the presence of a sixteen-year-old Devi dancing within her. It was her sixteenth puja. In 2016, I had a similar feeling and realized that another sixteen years had passed by. Time flies but the perfection of these moments remains the same. The scale of the puja at the ashram has had a quantum leap though, having to ensure arrangements for the tens of thousands of people who come there to stay and participate in the tradition. The kitchen has to stock itself way ahead to cook for all. Gurudev plans the menu himself. In 2015, for example, 30,000 kilos of rice, 3500 kilos of salt and 90,000 kilos of vegetables were consumed! Cooking every single meal for about 80,000 people can be quite a challenging task. How to imagine or judge the quantity of food needed? And it is not just one or two dishes that are prepared. There are sixteen to eighteen items on the menu as prasad on homa days. Over the past couple of years, mechanization has helped overcome some of the issues that come with scale, but in the initial days, everything was done by volunteers. People barely slept and were on their toes through the day and night.

The days of Navaratri is also the time of rains, leaky roofs, slushy pathways and power outages. There would always be more people than the ashram could accommodate. Sometimes, some volunteers have thought of restricting the entry of people into the ashram by granting admission on a first-come-first-served basis, but for Gurudev, the ashram is an open house where everyone is welcome. The team in charge of accommodation is always busy, making arrangements until the last moment. The challenge is that one can never anticipate how many guests will actually turn up. One needs to make myriad arrangements just for two or three guests, and imagine planning for thousands at a time! The preparations start months in advance and with each year the arrangements have improved with every small detail being attended to. But irrespective of the number of people, Gurudev personally meets each and every person who comes for the pujas during this auspicious time. The darshan lines are long and many, and go on for hours. The lines sometimes begin at the ashram gate and go all the way to the front of the yagyashala. Gurudev asks after everyone, making sure their needs are taken care of. At the end of the pujas, the pundits who come from other temples to participate tell me that they have never felt like this during any other puja. The Master's presence awakens a dimension that is unparalleled and inexplicable. Gurudev is one of the few enlightened masters who have kept this remarkable tradition alive.

A palm-leaf reader once came to the ashram on a Navaratri day to share what was revealed to him. He spoke of a conversation between a sage and his disciple. The sage said that all celestial beings come to the ashram to be in Gurudev's presence during Navaratri. The disciple asked what happens to other pujas if every celestial being were at the ashram. The sage replied that the pujas at the ashram are conducted for the benefit of humanity with no personal gain in mind. So when the celestial beings are at the ashram, the whole world benefits.

A tree may be laden with fruit but only those who can reach it can enjoy its sweetness. There are times when, out of love, trees let the fruits fall to the ground so that every child can pick them up and relish their taste. Similarly, the fruits of spiritual practices are not easily attainable even for advanced seekers on the path. But during times such as Navaratri, even the highest state of consciousness is easily attainable to us in the presence of a master.

It is September again. Now, when I drape the nine-yard silk around me, I feel its softness, the memory of my mother and the fact that it has witnessed more than three decades of pujas. The leela continues.

15

WHERE TIME FREEZES AND WISDOM FLOWS

THE COOL WATER gushed past my feet with an insistent tug as if it wanted to flow ahead. The great river was ancient, yet new. For thousands of years, her waters have absorbed the mantras chanted by sages on her banks. Small twigs and arti lamps floated past us with the river current. A few men and women took a deep breath and held their noses before immersing themselves in the holy water. The belief is that when they rise up from the water, their sins would be washed away. A small pool of water could get murky if too many people were to dip their feet in it, but not the Ganga. Nothing touched her. What a relief that was! Sages in the past chose their disciples carefully as they took on the karma of their disciples when they accepted them. And here was Gurudev with so many followers, and more and more were coming to him each day. I was deeply concerned about the possible consequences of his compassion. But the presence of the Ganga lifted the veil in my mind. Gurudev was not a small pond or lake. The words of Anandamayi Ma to Maharishi upon seeing a young Ravi flashed through my mind. 'You have brought me the Ganga.'

The majestic mountains of Rishikesh, the serene and vibrant Ganga, and the scintillating presence of the Master—the combination was ethereal. Each place has its own specialty and flavour, and Rishikesh is no different. We have had several advanced meditation programmes, Shivaratri celebrations and knowledge-sharing sessions in this sacred town. That particular day, we booked rooms at one of the ashrams by the riverside. We were woken up before dawn by the gentle flute music of one of our volunteers and we slowly trickled into the meditation hall to chant '*Om Namah Shivaya*'. The chanting was deeply meditative and evoked a subtle energy. After the immersion in the mantras came our immersion in the holy river, which was followed by yoga sessions. The hall had a small note outside that read, 'Leave your footwear and ego outside.'

Gurudev used to visit Rishikesh for a few weeks in March with our mother. As the period coincided with my children's exam schedules, I would usually stay back. One particular year, the exams got over earlier than usual and all of us travelled to Rishikesh together. Ajay, my elder son, had just completed his tenth grade and was made an Art Excel teacher (Art Excel is a programme developed by Gurudev for children) for this trip—he took care of all the smaller children. In the evenings, we would go for a stroll by the river with Gurudev. He would suddenly wade into the Ganga and everybody would follow suit irrespective of the attire they were dressed in. One could be dressed in a grand sari or a simple kurta—it did not matter.

My interest was also in the ashram kitchen. Amma would give a new recipe each day to the cooks who were also devotees.

We cut vegetables and made oval-shaped chappatis. Gurudev would also visit the kitchen often to check on what we were up to. He would pick up the giant ladle and stir the food. There was so much to do! Whatever we prepared got over quickly, and we had to make them all over again. Gurudev often recalls an old Hindi proverb, '*Man meetha tho jag meetha*', which means when there is sweetness in the mind, the world feels sweet too. The complaining aspect of our mind would go dormant in Gurudev's presence. One may have had minor complaints about small things or even big issues to deal with, but having experienced the positivity of his presence, it was tough for anyone to be negative again. If we take ten steps forward, we may go back by one or two steps, but never all the way back. By doing seva, one gains the merit to be in a positive environment.

When we returned to Bangalore, we would wonder if all of it was for real. The Ganga has been witness to several divine souls who have spent time on her banks. The river is called holy for a reason—it carries the sacred impressions of the sages. I feel their presence in the waters. As my mind flows along with the currents of the river, I also feel a dispassion arising within me. When Amma passed away, we performed her last rites on the ghats of the holy river. When I look at the Ganga and touch her waters now, I feel the presence of my mother.

On 9 November 1999, Amma breathed her last. At that time, Gurudev was in Varanasi, by the banks of Ganga. He was there for the consecration of a new idol of Devi Vishalakshi at the Shakti Peetha. Amma passed away at around 1.30 in the afternoon and Gurudev told us that the cremation should be completed by 5.30 in the evening. For a sanyasi, a bondage (of relationship and social norms that a son should follow) exists only as long as the body exists. After he heard the news, he took a dip in the Ganga and at 6.00 p.m. installed the idol at the temple.

Amma was dressed in a bright mustard yellow sari, which was one of her favourites. I had placed a large round maroon bindi on her forehead. She looked beautiful with a smile of contentment. Looking at her, I got a strong feeling to dress her up in red. She had purchased a new red Mysore silk sari, which she had hardly worn. I found it in her wardrobe and covered her with it. We had very little time and we took her to the ashram where everyone was waiting in queue, each with a flower in their hand to offer her. I went to Shakti Kutir and found a sandalwood garland there, which I placed around her neck. It was prasad from the Master.

We rushed back to the city soon after to complete the cremation. When it was over, Gurudev called me, and he said, 'You made her wear red. I was thinking of the same.' But how did he know about this? In the evening, he conducted a satsang with about eight thousand people as he did not want to disappoint those who had assembled for him. Some of the attendees told me that he was glowing like the sun. When they asked him about it, he said, 'I could feel the fire in every cell of my body.' Though the cremation was complete, he could still feel its heat. Gurudev came to Haridwar from Kashi and we also went there with the ashes. When we reached the place where Gurudev was waiting for us, he came forward and took the pot which held the ashes in his arms. The love with which he held it, as if holding Amma herself, is unforgettable. Tears flowed profusely from my eyes. A few months later, in

Italy, Gurudev saw someone holding a magazine with Amma's photo at a meditation course on it. The course was attended by about two thousand people. Gurudev said, 'There was a woman who loved me more than herself.' He glanced at the magazine, teary-eyed, and added, 'That is my mother.'

I miss Amma. During the months before her demise, it felt as if she had known that her time had arrived. During Navaratri that year, she made me and Anna take the puja sankalpas (the declaration of intention for doing a puja) with her and Pitaji. She started keeping me by her side as if she was handing over everything to me. After the Chandi puja got over, she complained of severe back pain. I felt that something was not okay. But like children who never want to see their parents ill, I told her, 'You will be fine. Just take rest.' That night, after the Rishi homa, I was with her. She started removing her jewellery one by one. Amma liked to wear her best jewellery on such occasions, but she took them off and gave them to me. 'Indha, nee vechukko (Here, you keep it)', she said. I did not want her to give me her jewellery for I liked seeing her bejewelled. Still, I wore a couple of the pieces thinking that perhaps she was finding them too heavy to wear. Though I was trying to explain away things, I had an inkling that things were not as they should be. I wanted to stay back with her at the ashram that night, but she sent me home saying, 'Go to your children. They will be waiting for you.' Early next morning, at 4.00, she had to be rushed to the hospital. Gurudev took her to the hospital himself and told me that her vijaya yatra (victory procession) had begun.

A few months later it was Karthik Purnima, a time when mothers would gift their daughters. Normally, Gurudev would be travelling at this time of the year, but he stayed at the ashram that year. When I visited him, he was waiting for me with gifts arranged the way my mother would have. I felt so grateful. He fulfils all roles and never lets you feel even an iota of emptiness.

Gurudev says that emptiness is a doorway between the material and spiritual worlds, and a place where one can understand the nature of the spirit. From emptiness begins fullness. On the one side of emptiness is misery; on the other side, joy. The Master helps one cross over. Gurudev could wade across a river, over slippery stones and through gushing water very comfortably. Not just during regular walks by the river, but even when he was visiting flood-affected areas. For people walking with him, it would get quite difficult for they had to keep pace with him while maintaining their balance. It looks so easy when one watches him from the banks. But when one tries to follow him, one wonders how he manages, that too without getting his dhoti wet or dirty!

After some of these walks, Gurudev would guide us into meditation. And I would feel as if there was a door opening, then another, and then yet another and so on as I moved from one loka (realm) to another. Normally, we are aware of only one level of existence. But there are several other higher planes as well. The scriptures have spoken about the different lokas—the pitr loka (of ancestors), the deva loka (of gods and other celestial beings) among others. I experienced the different realms in those few minutes. When one goes sightseeing, the vision is always outward. Here, the Master makes one go inward. In this inward journey, physical space also has a role to play, and the Master creates the right atmosphere. One could have all the ingredients to make tea, but without heat, the tea would taste bland. The presence of a master ignites the experience. And once one gets a glimpse of the subtle and the mystical, and gets attached to a place, he shifts it. Rishikesh is no longer a regular part of our March schedule any more. Gurudev never allows one to be attached to anything. The same mind can either make one entangled or free. When one feels a connection with one's self, there is no attachment. A sage is one who is firmly established in his or her self.

Many holy persons would visit Gurudev whenever he was at Rishikesh. They would meet and greet each other like they were friends. Pragyanandji Maharaj would call by every day. The conversations between them were most interesting. During discussions on the Upanishads, Gurudev would say, 'Tell us, Maharaj-ji, what does the scripture say?' Maharaj-ji always responded with great affection. Once he said, 'Gurudev, why should I search in the scriptures when I could get wisdom directly from you!'

Maharaj-ji also spoke about the importance of having meaningful names. He said that at the moment of death, if one remembers the Lord's name, one will attain a more peaceful state. People often remember their loved ones, and hence it is good to meaningful names. Gurudev smiled and said, 'Maharaj-ji, I get calls every day requesting me to name babies. I have come to remove all labels and identities, yet I have to do this too!'

They went on long walks by the Ganga or for a drive through the mountains. Sometimes, I would also get a chance to accompany them. During one such drive, someone commented that we were yet to spot an animal on the way.

Soon after, we stopped, and within moments, we heard some sounds. Gurudev said it was a herd of deer. And soon enough, a huge herd of deer came by, crossed the mountain path, stopped a while around us, and left. Then it was the turn of the monkeys—they came in groups, even bowed down to Gurudev and Maharaj-ji, and left. It was quite a sight! There were so many birds who came by one after the other. It was like a darshan line for them. What was in their minds? What did they feel? I really wonder at times. Animals are bound by nature but humans are bound by their cravings and aversions. Even positive feelings without knowledge can create negative feelings that are stifling, and bring bondage. But positive feelings with knowledge are liberating. Gurudev once put it lightly, 'When you follow fun, misery follows you and when you follow knowledge, fun follows you.'

16

ALL THE WORLD IS GURUDEV'S STAGE

IT WAS ANOTHER moment of serenity as I stood by the window of our hotel in California, looking at the gentle waves, hearing its whispers of love. Do they rise as part of a plan? Are they spontaneous, or an organized play of nature? How does Gurudev plan the things that he does, or decides on the places that he visits?

Gurudev walked into his kutir one day declaring, 'Devotees are dangerous!' He was chuckling as he repeated the statement. He had just returned from a two-day trip to Tamil Nadu, which had turned into quite an adventure. He was supposed to go to Neyveli for an event and fly back in a helicopter. But it started raining and the chopper was forced to land in a paddy field in the middle of nowhere. A few hundred villagers ran to the spot to investigate this unexpected vehicle and visitors. They took him to a small Devi temple nearby and talked about the problems they were facing, including the lack of rains. Gurudev assured the villagers that the problems were already being taken care of (the rains had come to begin with). By this time, a local Art of Living volunteer arrived at the spot with his car to escort Gurudev. It turned out that the volunteer was an administrative officer who was posted nearby. Gurudev apprised him of the difficulties that the villagers were facing and requested him to address their needs.

They decided to drive to Thiruvannamalai, where an advanced meditation programme was being conducted. When he arrived, the participants there could not believe their luck! They talked of how they had seen him flying en route to Neyveli and wishing that they could only make the copter land at their campsite. After interacting with them, Gurudev visited the local Shiva temple. At the temple, Shiva was being worshipped as the fire element. The temple priests had invited Gurudev a few months back to inaugurate the Kumbhabhishekam ceremony that happens once in twelve years. Gurudev's office had informed them that his schedule was packed and that it would not be possible for him to attend the ceremony. But here he was at the ceremony on the very same day! As per the tradition of the temple, the ceremony could only begin with the permission of a guru and providence ensured that it did. Walking out of the temple afterwards, he met some Kashmiri Muslim boys who were running a small handicrafts shop nearby. They came to him, thanked him, and said, 'We see what you are doing for Kashmir and have always wanted to meet you and thank you. We never thought we would get a chance like this.' After the meeting, he got into the car and started his journey back to the ashram. The volunteer accompanying him said that he had been wishing to take Gurudev on a long road trip and now his wish had been fulfilled. Could all of this have been planned?

Similarly, Gurudev went on an unplanned trip to Himachal

Pradesh once. 'I was supposed to inaugurate a power plant and return to Delhi by helicopter' he recounted, 'but the copter faced some technical issues and would not start. We proceeded by car and stopped at a place where close to five hundred people were waiting for me. They were unable to reach the venue on time because of a snowfall and were disappointed to have missed the event. But here I was with them! We drove further to the house of a devotee. In that house was an eighty-year-old lady who had wanted to come but could not as she was unwell. And a three-year-old child had dreamt that I would come there on 2nd March. Nobody paid any attention to the child, but I was there on that day. Perhaps this was the real plan!'

Sometimes, on Gurudev's unplanned trips, the person at the wheel would have scant idea about the destination of the trip. He would just receive instructions from time to time, and the drive would last until he was told to stop say in front of a small house on the outskirts of Bangalore. In one such instance, it turned out to be the residence of a farmer who was stunned to see Gurudev at his doorstep! Gurudev's articles were published regularly in the local newspaper in a section called 'Amritabindu', which means 'drops of nectar'. The farmer had collected all the articles and pasted them on the walls of his little house. He had been greatly wanting to meet Gurudev but was unable to leave his farmland unattended and find a means to travel to the city. But none of this mattered now, and he was overwhelmed by gratitude to receive the Master at his doorstep. But it was not just the people who knew him who were waiting for him.

When Gurudev went to Russia for the first time in May

1993, the organizers had somehow assumed that he would get a visa on arrival. The immigration officer, who had never met an Indian guru, was surprised when Gurudev told him, 'I have family waiting for me in Russia. I have to meet them.' Gurudev was soon in a taxi driving to meet those who had come to meet him. When they arrived at the venue of the talk, the hall was overflowing with hundreds waiting outside. Finally, Gurudev gave one talk inside the hall and another outside.

One of the Art of Living instructors, Scott Hague, asked Gurudev, 'How do you speak to so many people at a time?' 'I do not,' he replied, 'I never speak to a crowd. I speak to each person, one on one.'

The evening lecture in the city of Tula was not widely publicized and was announced just once on the radio, but even then over a hundred people attended. Gurudev began his talk and mentioned the word meditation. Immediately everyone started sitting upright. It was clear that they were there for meditation and not for an introductory lecture. Gurudev sensed this and said, 'Well, let's just start the course.' A gypsy woman from the audience came to him at the end of the programme and offered to read his palm. When she looked at his hand, she said, 'It's not possible, you have thousands of children!' Gurudev replied, 'Yes, I have a lot of children in every part of the world'.

After Russia, Gurudev left for Minsk, Belarus. Igor Soroko, the local Art of Living instructor there, was at the airport with a group of volunteers to receive him. It was raining, and Gurudev came out of the airport with an umbrella in his hand. Following their national tradition, they offered him bread and salt to show their hospitality. Gurudev took the loaf of bread respectfully, broke off a small piece and passed around the loaf, inviting everyone to share the bread. An evening talk was arranged at a large concert hall. When Gurudev entered the venue in his long white garments, the audience broke into applause. His smile lit up their faces. They were eager to listen to him, and he spoke in his soft, soothing voice.

'Let us look at how we live and in what way we spend our lives. On an average, a person lives for eighty years. We spend thirty years sleeping, and almost the same amount of time we spend working and in transport. About ten years are spent on eating and five years in the bathroom. How much time is left for giving love and smiling? Just a few years. In our entire life, this is the time that we really live. The rest of the time is spent on preparing to live.' Each person was listening to him attentively, every word unfolding something within them. 'Again and again we must ask ourselves: what do we really want in life? Do we want only food, money and success? Who are we? Where do we come from? What is the meaning of life?' When such questions arise, it means that the time has arrived. One is no longer satisfied with the superficial and seeks something deeper in life. Give yourself a pat on the back for this.'

At the end of the talk, he stood up and started chanting 'Om Namah Shivaya'. Spontaneously, everyone stood up and joined him. Gurudev started walking on the stage holding a large garland of flowers, from which he removed one flower after another and handed them over to the audience. Later, he left to go backstage, but people were still standing in the hallway unwilling to budge. Some minutes later, a long queue was formed in the corridor behind the room where Gurudev was. People clung to him when he reappeared to take leave. Igor said that even after Gurudev's car left the venue, the feelings of delight, love and gratitude were palpable among the people. They were sure that despite what the future held for them, they would be happy.

There is no dearth of excitement while travelling with Gurudev. In 1994, during a public talk in Paris, there was a young man seated in the first row who appeared to be quite agitated. He abruptly stood up in the middle of the talk and shouted at Gurudev, 'How can you talk of love and peace?' and walked out shaking with anger. Everyone in the audience felt relieved when he left, but Gurudev sent one of the volunteers after the young man, 'Let him have some time to settle down and then bring him back.' The man came in, and once again he stood up and shouted and walked out. Once again Gurudev sent a volunteer to fetch him back. The third time, the man started walking on to the stage. Everyone in the hall was quite nervous by then. But Gurudev was his usual calm, unshaken self. The man came to Gurudev, dropped to his knees, and placed his head on Gurudev's lap with tears flowing down his eyes. He looked completely at peace.

Once, in Baltimore, Gurudev was speaking on the importance of prayer at a public event. Suddenly, a man, almost seven feet tall and hefty looking, seated in the last row, started interrupting his speech. He said he found it laughable that people prayed and started guffawing in a threatening manner. Soon he started advancing towards Gurudev. Many of us panicked sensing the possibility of violence, but Gurudev signalled us to wait. He approached Gurudev, loomed over him and asked, 'Aren't you scared?' Gurudev just smiled and gently tapped on his forehead. The man collapsed to the ground weeping. He later did some basic and advanced programmes and started following Gurudev. The Yoga Sutras say that when people are established in non-violence, violence ceases to exist in their presence. I saw this happening in front of me.

The phenomenon of a 'guru' is rare and is not easy to understand, even more so outside India. In January 1996, Gurudev was in Zagreb, Croatia, for an evening of meditation. Two volunteers, Katja Gregl and Kiran, were with him. The Croatian War of Independence had just ended a year back, but the pain and sorrow of a people searching for a way out of the past were very evident. The hall allotted to us in Vatroslav Lisinski was not big enough to accommodate all of the eight hundred people who had turned up. After the event, Gurudev went out of the hall and blessed and embraced everyone one by one. It was not common for him to embrace people as he did in Croatia, but it was certain that his touch brought them immense relief. After this visit, he went to Slovenia. Hundreds thronged the World Trade Centre in Ljubljana to interact with him at an event titled 'Talk with a guru'. He said at the event, 'A student's job is to satisfy the teacher. But how can one satisfy someone who is already satisfied? If a guru is satisfied, then your growth is stunted. If a guru is unsatisfied, he's away from his true self. On the one hand, there is nothing that could inspire one to grow if a guru is satisfied. On the other, one cannot be a guru if one is unsatisfied. In short, one cannot be considered a guru if one is either satisfied or unsatisfied. So what is the answer?' His words stirred the audience into a state of wonder and admiration, and he was soon showered with flowers by the grateful crowd. Andrej Trampuz, an Art of Living teacher from Slovenia, recalled how the atmosphere was charged with gratitude and a celebratory mood.

Gurudev's travels are not always planned for a group. In the picturesque Umbria region of Italy, Gurudev decided to climb on top of a hill to go to a little church. When Gurudev arrived, the priest was moved to tears. He said that the night before he had dreamt of Gurudev (he had never met Gurudev before) and that in his church all masters from all traditions were welcome.

Once, while in Italy, Gurudev was in a car when he suddenly asked the driver to stop the vehicle. He got off, and to everyone's surprise, went to a thicket nearby and came back with another man. It turned out that the man was suicidal. He said that he was a scuba diver who had experienced samadhi, a state of meditative consciousness, while he was deep in the sea some time back. He was unable to experience it again and nothing made sense to him any more. The man was praying to God to save him if he really existed and cared for him. At just that moment, Gurudev found him.

Once, Gurudev advanced the date of his trip to Sofia, Bulgaria, by four days. But on the previously specified date, a performance of over two hundred bagpipers was already planned with halls booked and tickets sold. Now everything would have to be reorganized. Konstantin Dragov, an Art of Living volunteer in Bulgaria, was quite worried at first. He told me that Bulgaria was not like India. In Europe, such abrupt changes in plans are unheard of, but the necessary changes were, nevertheless, made. The programmes were a big success and people who participated in the advanced meditation course enjoyed it in the presence of the Master himself for three days.

The volunteers returned home feeling contented after bidding farewell to Gurudev at the airport. The same night Bulgaria witnessed an earthquake—one of the biggest in its history. If the programme was planned as per the initial schedule, there would have been no programme at all. Interestingly, the newspapers reported no casualities even though the quake happened at night when people were sleeping.

In another instance, Gurudev decided to conduct a yagya in Bali, Indonesia. The Indonesian organizers proposed that the programme should be postponed by a week because of local festivals, but Gurudev insisted on his dates. It was called the Light of Peace yagya and was conducted in an open area. Seating arrangements were made all around for the participants to witness the pujas. As soon as the yagya began, it started raining. The Balinese people consider rain as an auspicious sign, but soon it started pouring heavily. What was amazing was that the area of the yagya remained relatively unaffected by the rain. After the completion of the yagya, the chief priest of Bali shared with us that Rishi Markendeya had performed the same yagya two thousand years back to shield Bali against harmful forces. Around the same time, a Chinese clairvoyant came to meet Gurudev. He had the ability to correctly decipher what people were thinking at a particular moment. Some people wanted to know if he could read Gurudev's mind as well. But he could not. They asked, 'So is Gurudev too powerful for you to penetrate his mind?' He replied, 'No, there are no barriers. I cannot read his mind because he has no mind!' So, where is the Master's plan made if there is no mind?

As rare as it is, this 'no-mindedness' could be infectious. During the International Women's Conference that was held at the ashram in 2005, Ruth Ostrow, a senior journalist and video producer from Australia, had come as a speaker and wanted to interview Gurudev for an Australian newspaper. She wanted to hear his views on politics, Hinduism, the rise of western Buddhism, the role of women in Indian life, spiritualism and, finally, the meaning of life itself. She had come fully prepared. But the moment Gurudev said, 'Yes Ruth, ask me' her mind went blank! Gurudev was smiling and the whole room was quiet. She looked as if she would panic any moment when another American journalist who was in the room reassured her. 'He does this to all of us. You come prepared with questions and he zaps you out and makes you forget them!' Everyone laughed. I am not sure if Ruth found this funny though. I have seen many coming to him full of questions in their mind only to forget them when they actually meet him! The next day Ruth shared one of her experiences with me. 'Everyone was giving Gurudev flowers, and he would hand them over to people with his blessings. As I watched him, all I could do was worry that I did not have a story yet. He came to me and picked out a flower that I thought he was going to give me, but instead he tapped me on the head. I jumped back in surprise. He laughed, and I could not help but laugh too. And a chorus of laughter ensued. Everybody laughed like happy children, innocent and playful, like the Master himself. I felt a rush of joy. And as my soul awakened, my mind finally went quiet. "Ruth, do you understand now?" he asked, smiling at me. "Yes, Gurudev", I answered, and since then I have never forgotten.'

Some moments can never be forgotten. There was a devotee in Delhi in whose house Gurudev was staying. She was peeling oranges for Gurudev, seated on one side, and I sat facing her. Gurudev was talking to the people in the room. She was looking at him, smiling and peeling the oranges and throwing the peels in a small container she had kept to collect the waste. With great devotion, she then offered the peels to Gurudev. I looked at him and looked back at her. She was clueless and I was speechless! His eyes twinkled with laughter as he pointed out the sweetness in the orange peels given with love! Everyone was in splits. The lady was profusely apologetic yet humbled by the unconditional acceptance and love from her guru. When and where a person meets their master is certainly part of a plan, but I wonder if eating orange peels is part of the plan too!

It is not always the guru who gets to savour all the tasty treats. We were in Pretoria, staying at Art of Living teacher Niyati's father's house. It was breakfast time and there were about thirty people with us. Fruits, bread and many types of pickles were all arranged on the table. Drinking tea was a very important part of the breakfast. South Africans pride themselves on the quality and flavour of their tea. Gurudev had met with the president of the country a day back and Hema, a local volunteer, was very keen on updating him on the developments post the meeting. She stood near Gurudev with her cup of tea, and as she was updating him, she accidentally took a spoonful of fresh pickle and mixed it with her tea. As the aroma of the tea intensified, she reached out for another spoonful. 'They loved everything Gurudev. They said they have never had such an experience and wanted more time with you.' My eyes widened as I saw her fetching more pickle. I looked at Gurudev and he was smiling with a sparkle in his eyes. As he was asking her a few questions, she took a few sips of her tea. I watched her keenly as her taste buds started sending frantic messages to her brain about the unusual taste. Although she was having some difficulty, she was far too focused on her updates to care! Who cares how the tea tastes when one is with one's guru. Yet, it was equally important to finish the cup of tea. Updates over, Gurudev asked her, 'How was your tea?' 'A little spicy ...' and her eyes shifted from Gurudev to the rest of us, who were keenly watching her. Suddenly, everyone in the room burst out laughing.

We stayed in Pretoria for three days. On the last day, Gurudev suddenly got up and went to the adjacent room, where Vinod Menon and Swami Brahmatej, among others, stayed. He picked up a packet that was lying on the table and handed it over to me for safekeeping. The packet, containing Ceylon tea, was addressed to Gurudev. Vinod had not passed the gift over as Gurudev does not drink tea. But the person who gave it (Niyati's father) did not know that. 'He gave it to me with so much devotion that I was forced to steal it back!' said Gurudev. Pickled tea, a stolen tea bag—these are some of the spicy memories we have of our devotees!

Gurudev says, 'Devotion is a gift. One cannot take credit for it. If one is devoted, it is a blessing.' People come to him asking for blessings for things ranging from health, jobs to marriage and even a fruitful trip to the shopping mall! But the people of Mongolia were different altogether. There was a long line of parents who requested Gurudev to bless their babies for enlightenment! It is no surprise that almost 60 per cent of the Mongolian population has learnt the Sudarshan Kriya and meditates regularly.

Once, a mother and her three-year-old were waiting in line for darshan at an advanced meditation programme in the Bangalore ashram. The child asked its mother, 'What happens when Gurudev hugs someone?' The mother said, 'You will get a chance soon, and then tell me what happened to you.' The little boy, after his turn, said, 'Amma, there was nobody, I felt like I was hugging myself.'

The boy's experience reminded me of a poem by Gurudev.

If I had to promise you something, what would it be?
I can't promise that you will always be comfortable
Because comfort brings boredom and discomfort.
I can't promise that all your desires will be fulfilled

Because desires whether fulfilled or unfulfilled bring
    frustration.
I can't promise there will always be good times
Because it's the tough times that make us appreciate joy.
I can't promise riches, fame or power
Because they can all be pathways to misery.
I can't promise we'll always be together
Because it is separation that makes togetherness so
    wonderful.

Yet if you are willing to walk with me
If you are willing to value love over everything else
I promise this will be the most enriching and fulfilling life.
I promise your life will be an eternal celebration,
I promise I will cherish you more than a king cherishes
    his crown,
I shall love you more than a mother loves her newborn.
If you are willing to walk into my arms,
If you are willing to live in my heart,

You will find the one you have waited for forever
You will meet yourself in my arms
I promise.

Children are very sensitive. They experience and learn values very quickly. Cleanliness is one such value that Gurudev has instilled in my children. When he used to visit us, he would inspect their rooms, check on even the window grilles for dust and grime, and appreciate the way they maintained the house. Inculcating the habit of cleanliness was achieved through fun and the boys thoroughly enjoyed it.

Once we were cleaning Shakti Kutir when Gurudev was away. I was checking the expiry dates of the Ayurvedic medicines and creams that were kept in his room and found two tubes of Fair & Lovely (a fairness cream) that were quite old. So I threw them away. When Gurudev returned, he glanced around his room and asked Zaver Patel, a volunteer at the ashram, 'There were two tubes of Fair & Lovely here. Did you throw them away?' Zaver did not know anything about them. I told Gurudev that I had cleaned up the room. 'Do not throw anything away without asking me,' he said. He never used the cream but still kept them in his room. Gurudev is dusky in complexion, and when he once joked about it, a devotee from Mumbai had given him the two tubes of cream with a quip, 'Gurudev, you are fair and lovely twice over!' The tubes were kept in remembrance of her. Perhaps she also needed Gurudev's attention at that time—at least, that is how I understand it. I called her up and informed her of what had happened and asked her to get two new tubes of the cream the next time she was around!

A family from north India had once come to Gurudev

to receive his blessings for their daughter, who was about to get married. They had brought two big boxes of dry fruit for Gurudev. Once they left, Gurudev got up for lunch. Zaver and I followed him, carrying one box each. Zaver suddenly handed over the second box to me and said, 'With one, get another one free.' Gurudev, who was just a few feet ahead, turned with a smile and said, 'When you are all with the one, everybody is free!' That was his plan for us—to enable us to be free, to leap joyously from the world of dry fruit to the fruits of human life.

Speaking of fruits, I am reminded of the tastiest pulao that I have ever had. We were once at Lake Tahoe, Sierra Nevada, for an advanced meditation programme. Gurudev decided to stay a day longer than what was decided in the beginning. The participants also changed their plans accordingly and decided to stay back. Our camp was far away from any township and, therefore, it was difficult to arrange adequate provisions. It was going to be lunch time, and we had to arrange food for everybody. The organizers were planning to order pizza, which would have taken a minimum of three hours to arrive. At that point, Gurudev came into the kitchen and checked the provisions that were available. He asked for the largest vessel that we had and put all the rice that was available in it. He made us cut whatever vegetables and fruits that were left and added them into the cooking pot. We handed him the box of spices—turmeric, cinnamon, black pepper—and he just took a handful of each of the spices and added them into the mix. He then added water and salt, covered the lid and said, 'Come, let us meditate.' Soon after, an inviting fragrance wafted through the air and into the hall. Gurudev went into the kitchen, brought a vessel full of pulao and started serving it to everyone. It tasted heavenly! People asked for a second and third serving, and some even took small servings home as prasad. Not only was the pulao delicious, but there was enough and more for everybody! As Gurudev once told us, 'When you walk the path with me, there won't be any lack.'

I know some of our instructors who have worked and continue to persevere in Iraq, which has been under siege for long. They have no fear and lack nothing as their connection with their guru is a source of unending strength for them. Gurudev has visited Iraq three times as of now. Many a time, he visits a certain country because the head of the country wants him there. However, Gurudev's visits do not remain confined to high-level meetings—he goes to problem areas, meets with the people who are affected, and provides hope and solace to them. When he is on such trips, we come to know of his plans only once they are executed, our initial sources of information being news channels, followed by first-hand accounts from Gurudev once he is back at the ashram. Perhaps he never tells us anything beforehand as he knows we would worry for his safety. In an interview with CNN on his visit to Iraq, he said, 'In most other parts, people suffer due to natural calamities. Here people are suffering due to their anger and frustration. It is a man-made calamity.' He taught the Iraqis meditation and breathing techniques to help them overcome the trauma of war.

Due to an ongoing government curfew, he met the leaders at night and impressed upon them the value of dialogue as a means to dispel mistrust. He said, 'I cannot even ask you how you are as I have seen how much trauma you have undergone.

Iraq deserves peace. That is why I have left everything and come here.' Gurudev was hosted in the green zone with armed security offered by the government. But he felt a pull towards the red zone, to have dialogue with the people who needed it the most. The local organizers were resistant to the idea. 'I have not come here to just sit in the safety of my hotel,' he said, 'I have come to give the message of peace to each and every person.' The next morning, he set out on his journey to Najaf, a province in the red zone. He had to change cars twice for security reasons. One could not even drive one's car on a straight course in the area due to the danger of gunfires. Gurudev visited madrasas and spoke about the teachings of Mahatma Gandhi. He met with imams and requested them to give non-violence a chance. A Red Crescent official who accompanied him on the trip said, 'Until now, we have only known the art of dying. You have brought into Iraqi life the art of living!'

Inspired by Gurudev, fifty young Iraqi men and women came to the Bangalore ashram to train as instructors of yoga and meditation and launch peace activities once they were back with their people. Gurudev visited Iraq again within the next two years. The third time, he organized a peace conference in Erbil, Kurdistan, a violence-hit province. He said, 'Peace conferences are being held where there is peace. I want to do this conference in the middle of conflict, where it is needed.' He visited Yazidi camps in Sinjar Mountains and met with Kurds, Christians and Arabs. One camp housed children who had lost one or both of their parents. They came running to him and surrounded him. The local people said that they were smiling for the first time in months. They came and hugged him. He blessed the children, one by one, and told them they would all find a good home and be taken care of. With his guidance, food supplies were air-dropped in the mountains and over two hundred girls were saved from trafficking. Nouri al-Maliki, the former prime minister of Iraq, said, 'There are big powers who have the might, but they are unable to unite the hearts and minds of people. This work can only be done by a spiritual leader.'

When Gurudev was invited as the keynote speaker at the Evangelical Church Day event in Frankfurt, in 2001, addressing thousands of Christians, he said, 'Religion is like a banana peel and its values and spirituality the fruit inside. Today we have thrown away the fruit and are holding on to the peel. We need to focus on common values and then we will be able to see that we all belong.' Over the years, Gurudev has met with leaders of all communities and religions to open up inter-faith dialogues and bring inter-faith harmony.

When Gurudev travelled to Japan for the first time, he stayed at a Buddhist monastery in an island in Tokyo. Scott Hague had accompanied him. The immaculate monastery had lovely gardens full of songbirds. The rooms were separated by thin paper walls, and everyone slept Japanese style on floor mats. Scott received a group that had come to meet Gurudev at the train station. As they walked through the tiny overcrowded streets, Scott shared with the group his personal experiences with Gurudev. When the group arrived, Gurudev resorted to silence. Scott introduced everyone, trying to get the conversation rolling. But Gurudev just kept smiling in a state of bliss. Finally, one of the group members started weeping, and then another. No one spoke. The room was filled with an intensely overwhelming sense of harmony. After a while, Gurudev took leave. On their way back to the train station, the group members said, 'We've never experienced anything like this in our lives. Could we come back again tomorrow?' They had appreciated the silence and the grace surrounding Gurudev. The next evening they returned with their friends and this time Gurudev conversed with them and also gave a talk. The morning Gurudev was supposed to leave, he rose early to join the monks for morning chants. The monks would customarily bow before a statue of Buddha after the incantations. Yet, on this particular morning, they all turned to Gurudev. The head monk said, 'We bow to the divine, and this morning we see the divine's presence not only in the statue of Buddha but in front of us as well.' They all bowed in respect.

Many governments and leaders have honoured Gurudev. I feel proud looking at the work that he has done. And when I express this, he simply says, 'The world venerates wisdom.' Guru Tattva is the dawning of wisdom in our life. Gurudev says, 'Your own life is your guru. The Guru is not a school teacher from whom you learn something and then go away. Life and Guru are inseparable.' At a satsang, a participant asked, 'Am I connected to you?' Gurudev said, 'No, I am not connected to you. I was never separate to be connected.'

Perhaps this oneness that he feels with everyone is what pulls people to him and in turn pulls him back to people. When Gurudev visited South Korea, the Korean newspapers mistakenly carried the wrong time of his programme. Cecilia Angelini, the organizer, realized this barely a few hours before the event. When she called the venue, there were just fifty people who had managed to arrive. But Gurudev was still prepared to go. How could she have not noticed this earlier? When they were near the venue, Gurudev requested her to go around the block once more before entering the venue. It was a five-minute drive, but when they were near the gate, there was a rush of people trying to get a spot because the hall was chock-a-bloc with over five hundred people!

When he was in Argentina for the first time, there was heavy rain when he arrived. This was a Catholic country and the concept of a guru was unknown to the people there. The organizers had booked an auditorium but were worried that no one would turn up. With a few minutes left for the talk, people trickled in and soon all seats were occupied by curious Argentines raring to meet and experience a spiritual guru. At the end of the talk, they queued up to receive a hug from 'the man of light' as they called him. Similarly, in 2000, at the UN Millennium World Peace Summit in, a group of shaman priests surrounded him in the lobby of the hotel where he was staying and hailed him as 'the man of light'.

The 'man of light' once decided to visit the 'no man's land' in Sri Lanka. In 2006, the government of Sri Lanka requested him to facilitate peace talks between the then Sri Lankan president Mahinda Rajapaksa and the LTTE chief Velupillai Prabhakaran. Gurudev left Colombo at around 4 in the morning for the meeting. Government personnel accompanied him until the border of the LTTE territory. Then he proceeded across the 'no man's land' in a car driven by a volunteer and accompanied by two Art of Living instructors. The land was open, dry, constantly under the surveillance of the LTTE, and had perhaps seen more bullets than rains. Having crossed the 'no man's land', he waited at the UN checkpost and sent word for the gates to be opened. After an hour or so, the passports were checked and they proceeded to Kilinochchi, the then administrative centre of the LTTE. The guards at the watch tower, the LTTE officers checking the papers, and the soldiers at the guesthouse—most of them were in their twenties or early thirties. The town was awash with posters of martyred LTTE soldiers. When Gurudev arrived in Kilinochchi, he was told that he was one among the few who could cross into the region without being greeted by bullet fires. Gurudev was then asked to wait about a kilometre away from the LTTE chief's residence. However, after having committed to come, Prabhakaran did not turn up and sent his deputies instead.

Gurudev emphasized upon them the need for a different approach to achieve the LTTE's goal and distributed some clothes and medicines, which he had carried from India. Those who helped set up the meeting apologised and shared their worry that this was the last opportunity for their people and now a disaster was waiting to happen. 'Thousands of lives could have been saved if Prabhakaran had come,' Gurudev later said. He never left any stone unturned in his efforts for a peaceful resolution. The Sri Lankan army abandoned the ceasefire pact and began a military offensive against the LTTE in 2008. In 2009, in the heat of the battle, Gurudev visited Sri Lanka again to meet people displaced during the war. Post the war, Art of Living was one among the very few NGOs that the Sri Lankan government invited for rehabilitation work in the country. Our instructors and volunteers spent days there to conduct trauma relief camps for the thousands of refugees.

Dan Shilon, an Israeli television host, told Gurudev during his visit to Jerusalem in 2012, 'You must be very disappointed.

The world is not going your way.' Gurudev replied, 'Do I look disappointed? I have patience and perseverance.' Shilon went on, 'You measure success by a smile and you are smiling all the time, yet the world is not smiling.' Gurudev said, 'Doctors have a job to treat patients. If doctors fall sick, there is no hope for patients. As reformers, if we lose our smile, we cannot bring smile to others.'

During his trip to Israel, he visited the Dome of the Rock mosque. Gurudev had covered his head in reverence and bowed down in front of the foundation stone at the centre of the mosque. Hassan Tafti, who had accompanied him, touched by this act, was curious to know why he chose to do this. Gurudev said, 'If a stone can inspire faith in a person, it is worthy of our respect.' This cleared the lingering doubts in Hassan's mind regarding idol worship. Hassan added, 'Gurudev has paid his respects at the Wailing Wall too. He was so involved that he did not come across as someone practising another religion. Gurudev respects all religions equally. This was very touching for me.'

In 2009, Gurudev was invited to speak at a programme entitled 'Facing Tomorrow', which was part of the Presidential Conference organized in Jerusalem and attended by thirteen heads of state and three thousand and five hundred delegates. The conference was held as part of Israel's sixtieth anniversary celebrations. At the event Gurudev said, 'When I was coming to Israel they asked me, "Do you want the Israeli stamp on your passport?" I said yes. They added, "Don't get it stamped on your passport. Take a separate sheet. It is done even at the embassy. You could get the visa stamped on a separate piece of paper. Otherwise, you may face problems going to

Arab countries." I emphasized that I wanted the stamp on my passport. The world is my family. I am committed to Israel. I am connected to Jewish people as I am to the people of Iran, Iraq and Pakistan. We need to break this narrow mindedness and make people realize that we are all part of a one-world family.'

During one of his trips to Russia, Gurudev visited cities across all eleven time zones and everywhere he was on time! No jet lag, no tiredness—he was ever ready to meet the people who were waiting for him. During one of those trips, a last-minute visit to Moscow was announced. The organizers booked a hall the night before for an event scheduled for 9.00 the next morning. In the bitter cold, while it was still snowing, people were in queue waiting to get a place inside the hall. Stanislav Guemes, our Russian volunteer, said that people in Russia do not do this even for the most popular rockstars in their country. He added, 'I always tell people to just travel with Gurudev once and see for themselves that there is something beyond the ordinary at work.' A curious devotee once asked Gurudev, 'How do you decide where to go?' He said, 'I just go wherever my devotees call me.' Someone else asked, 'You do so much travel and so much work. When do you rest?' He said, 'Between lifetimes.'

17

WISDOM FOR BREAKFAST

I AM SITTING on my swing having a breakfast of piping hot idlis, chutney and sambar. Most mornings fresh idlis are made at home. Their taste and texture, the way they melt in my mouth, their spongy, circular shape stay the same but the idlis never happen to be 'like yesterday's'. Two sunrises are never the same; each leaf of the same branch is unique. Our consciousness loves newness. Every time I meditate, it is a new experience for me. 'One more idli for you?' My musings are interrupted by my cook. 'Yes, just one more.' Someone recently told me that idlis are among the most nutritious and wholesome foods. Gurudev often says, 'When one can accept food and music from all across the world, why not wisdom?'

Once Ayatollah Khomeini's assistant, an elderly gentleman of about seventy-eight years, visited the ashram. He asked Gurudev, 'I have a serious question, a serious doubt. I have been asking this all my life but couldn't find an answer. Hope you can help me.' Gurudev said, 'Yes, please tell me.' He said, 'How can there be many correct answers to one question? If the truth is singular, the answer should also be singular. There cannot be two different right answers. And if there is just one right answer, having so many religions makes no sense. There can be only one right religion. How can all paths be correct? If the truth is singular, all scriptures cannot be right.' This was a very convincing argument. Gurudev answered, 'See, to reach this place, there are many ways. One could travel straight and reach here. One could go straight and turn right or go straight and turn left and still reach this place. It depends on where you are.' He continued, 'In India, there is an ancient thought that says, "Let knowledge flow from all sides." The truth is one but perceived in many ways. *Ekam sat vipra bahudha vadanti*, which means that the truth is singular, but the intelligent express it in many ways.' The gentleman, pleased with the answer, thanked Gurudev.

But he was not the only one to seek this answer. The understanding of truth as multidimensional is a paradigm shift in perception for many. Gurudev was invited to address the Third World Congress of Imams and Rabbis for Peace hosted by the UNESCO in Paris. At the conference, when the imams and rabbis disagreed, they did not mind expressing their disagreements. The session was also a stage for exchanging ideas to mend Israel-Palestine relations. When Gurudev spoke, people hailed it as a voice of spiritual peacebuilding. He shared his vision of a one-world family, an idea that could be traced back to several hundred years. 'The wise see commonality across religions but also celebrate differences. If there is extremism in even one part of the world, the world is not a safe place. People who think that only their religion can lead them to heaven create hell for everybody. First and foremost, we are part of one divinity and life. Only then we are part of particular nations or religions. The identity of humanness should prevail over all other identities. We should teach our children a little bit more about all the religions in the world, so that they grow up with a broad vision and a sense of cultural belongingness. Multicultural and multi-religious education is most essential. Then we will not find any fanaticism in the world.'

In March 2012, while being interviewed by *The Daily Beast* in the context of the Taliban announcing that it had pulled out of its peace talks with the US, Gurudev stated that he would like to initiate a dialogue with the Taliban in Pakistan. At a time when very few people were willing to mediate, he said, 'We'll go in with an open mind to find out who they are and what their problems and intentions are—this has always been my approach. All those who fight have their fears and concerns; they want to feel valuable. Conflict rises in the head, in the individual, and only then it spreads to the community.' He talked of a humane, personal approach that could succeed at a point when official diplomatic efforts were breaking down.

When Gurudev was invited to speak at a gathering of fifty former heads of state at the Interfaith Council in Vienna in 2014, he was introduced as an expert on mediation, not just meditation! Gurudev was also invited to the Vatican the same year. The bishops received Gurudev with great respect and sought his advice on bringing all faiths together to work against poverty and especially child trafficking. This was his second visit to the Vatican. His first visit in 1984 was at a time when there was resistance to yoga and meditation to such a degree that it was even considered taboo. However, Gurudev's constant efforts have brought about a phenomenal transformation in how these practices are now perceived globally.

In December 2014, the UN declared 21 June as International Yoga Day. Soon after, Gurudev was invited to the European Parliament as a special guest to address the parliament on 'The Yoga Way'. One of the dignitaries remarked that with over five hundred attendees, the Parliament had never been so full. 'From Gross Domestic Product (GDP), we are moving towards Gross Domestic Happiness (GDH). Yoga could aid in this transformation,' stated Gurudev. On 21 June 2015, he was at the UN headquarters in New York organizing a yoga session, and followed it up with a visit to the Times Square where thousands were waiting for him. He had taken the ancient practice from a small house in Jayanagar to the European Parliament, the UN, and to millions of people worldwide. When Gurudev met with a journalist from *The Wall Street Journal* at New York's Lincoln Center, he was asked 'Is the practice of yoga religious?' He said, 'Yoga, Ayurveda, mathematics, the names of some English months ... they all originate from Vedic traditions. But there is no belief system attached to all of this; it does not bar you from believing in a specific form of God or even impose that you must believe in God. Newton discovered the law of gravitation. But that's not considered a Christian law.' Addressing a large audience, he added, 'Yoga suits today's busy world because we don't have time to practise much yet want the best results.'

Yoga is not just a set of asanas or a type of physical exercise but is a kind of union. Gurudev says, 'It is like a wave uniting with its depth.' Doing asanas with the guidance of Gurudev is a very unique experience. In my teens and even after my marriage, I used to go to a nearby yoga school for my practice. However, when I practised under Gurudev, the level of experience was higher. For every stretch taken, he furthered one's awareness of every organ where a change was effected. Usually, one is aware of only the breathing technique or the sensation provided by a stretch. But how about being aware of one's pulse, the stomach's stretching, or the spleen's compression? I had never really even thought about the spleen before! Often, at the end of meditation, a generic instruction is given to pay attention to the body. But the level of awareness inculcated by Gurudev opens up a new dimension. He says that all yogic postures were realized spontaneously by sages who were immersed in deep meditation. It is possible that one could go into a state of meditative samadhi in any posture. It seems unthinkable being in samadhi while doing a sirsasana (headstand) or a bhujangasana (cobra pose), but it is very much possible. Gurudev also connects each posture to its inspiration in nature. In essence, a simple marjariasana (cat stretch) could make one feel connected to the totality around us and unwind one's mind to the infinite presence.

The nature of a joyful person is to share, which is made possible through service. In 2012, on the occasion of its sixty-fifth anniversary, Nyenrode Business University, based in the Netherlands, conferred an honorary doctorate on Gurudev. The university recognized him as one of the most influential spiritual leaders of our times and stated, 'His spiritual knowledge, charitable work and teachings have united millions of students and world leaders across all continents. His pragmatic approach towards spirituality has led to a greater awareness within small and larger organizations throughout the whole world.' At the award ceremony, Gurudev remarked, 'In today's business world there is a lot of uncertainty. Business depends on social and political values, and spirituality can add the much-needed strength and enthusiasm into the equation.' When Art of Living volunteers congratulated Gurudev, he smiled and said, 'It is a period of celebration now, but actually this honour is adding to the responsibility of making this world a better place.'

A few years earlier, Gurudev was invited to speak at the World Economic Forum in Davos. At the forum, a round table conference was held in which various heads of states and CEOs of large business empires participated. The conference was divided into groups, and in each group about ten leaders presented their respective views. Gurudev listened patiently to each member in his group and was the last to speak. He presented his talk on the five principles of happy living, which he had been sharing at various happiness programmes organized by Art of Living. The group was of the opinion that what Gurudev shared was a mantra for success in the coming times. They unanimously chose him to represent the views of the group to the entire gathering, and when he did the presentation, the entire room gave him a standing ovation.

Gurudev says, 'Trust is the breath of business, ethics its limbs, and to uplift the human spirit is its goal.' In May 2006, on the occasion of Gurudev's fiftieth birthday, Nirj Deva, a member of the European Parliament, approached him and asked if the 'Corporate Culture and Spirituality' conferences held in Bangalore since 2003 could be organized at the European Parliament. Gurudev agreed to the suggestion, and when volunteers asked him about the particulars of the conference, he said, 'Have people discuss if ethics and business are contradictory or complementary.'

We were all inspired to help, but organizing an event of that scale was a major challenge for our comparatively smaller team in Europe. They sought the help of one of the best conference organizers in Germany but he asked for nine months' time and 700,000 euros for the job. We had neither the time nor the budget, and the team came back to Gurudev for his guidance. In his usual style he said, 'Just do it, and it will all happen.' Four months later, we organized the first World Forum for Ethics in Business at the European Parliament, which was attended by over 300 delegates.

In June 2014, Gurudev visited the American Enterprise Institute. He was visiting the Washington D.C. based think tank to speak on the idea of human flourishing. Arthur Brooks, the president of the institute, asked Gurudev, 'Is it true that compassion and free enterprise are intertwined and one helps build on the other?' Gurudev responded, 'Whether capitalism, communism, socialism or whatever "ism" it is, no "ism" will work without humanism.' He added, 'I don't see any conflict between capitalism and compassion. Rather, capitalism can flourish well with compassion, and compassion can only happen with people who can afford to show compassion and do something about it.'

Gurudev's interventions are, however, not limited to business but also extend to areas as diverse as sports. Once, in Portugal, the volunteer who was driving Gurudev to one of the events was getting anxious as Portugal was playing a very important football match. He asked Gurudev if he could turn on the radio to follow the match commentary. But all that could be heard on the radio for several minutes was the noise of the match. Since nothing significant was happening, the volunteer proceeded to turn off the radio, but Gurudev requested that the volume be turned up and he listened to the commentary earnestly. The event in Portugal was near the Atlantic Ocean at sunset. Gurudev started his speech that day with the following quip, 'In this life we make war as if it were a game, and we play a game as if it were a war.'

Two years later, when FIFA was rocked by allegations of corruption, Gurudev held the 'World Forum for Ethics in Sports' at the FIFA headquarters in Zurich in 2014. In his address, he said that sports are a way to channelize the tremendous energy of youth. If we replaced guns with a football or a cricket bat, that would be a step towards global peace. He shared a personal anecdote and talked about the spirit of sports. 'Once, a little boy was sad and upset at losing a race. I said, "Look, you lost the race, but isn't the person who won the race your friend? Are you not happy that your friend has won? Suppose you won the race, and your friends were unhappy about it, would you like it?" This question made the little boy think about his loss in a different manner. In a game, somebody would win, but that ought to be an occasion of celebration for everybody. If that spirit is lacking, then it is no longer a game but a war or a competitive business. Infusing this spirit in sports is important to uplift human consciousness.'

Gurudev has maintained that whether one wins or makes others win, in both cases one is a winner and never a loser. He has always created win-win situations everywhere. If at all people should lose something, it should be their problems and worries.

18

THE WORLD IS ONE FAMILY

THE MONSOON SHOWERS have arrived. Looking out of the window, it is such a joy to watch the rain drops bathing the mangoes and listen to their pitter-patter on the roof. They have come all the way from the sky and are so close now that one could touch them and feel connected to the clouds and the sky. By immersing in the feeling, one could imagine living amid the clouds without in the least being cloudy minded!

During spring 2010, at a public gathering in the Netherlands, Gurudev presented the audience with a question, 'How and where should we celebrate the thirtieth anniversary of Art of Living?' Ideas started flowing in, and some of our volunteers suggested a plan that looked a little far-fetched in the beginning. They wanted to celebrate the big day in a stadium in Europe. Gurudev was ever ready as usual and said, 'Yes, this is what we will do!' And preparations started in full swing for an event at the historic Olympic Stadium in Berlin.

The event was scheduled for July, just a few days before the World Cultural Festival (WCF) in July 2011. Gurudev requested Stephan Chopard, an Art of living teacher from

Switzerland, to buy shawls for everybody, but we were expecting a sunny day for the programme. But it turned out that the day received an unusual out-of-season shower, and the shawls were of great help during the chilly rain. Although it was pouring, not one person in the 70,000-strong stadium left the venue. Hundreds of umbrellas opened up, covering the entire seating area of the stadium. Normally, when it rains, one prefers to stay inside, but this day I was standing in the open with the rains enveloping me. It was wonderful feeling the blessings from the skies showering over me. Although it was cold, there was so much warmth around me, being connected to people from 150 countries! The artists danced and sang with abandon as if inspired by the rain. The dancers from Russia performed 'Swan Lake', a ballet, literally in a puddle of water! The raindrops glistened on their faces as brightly as their sparkling costumes. Little droplets flew from the tips of their fingers as they gracefully moved around, with each movement enhancing the whole performance. The dancers from Bulgaria skipped and hopped on the wet and slippery grass and matched the rhythm of the drops falling on the earth as their lead artist sang a song on water. She was a skilled drummer, too, and water drops flew from her drumsticks like flashes of lightning. The grand finale song was called 'Colours of the rainbow'.

The volunteers were wondering as to why the rain did not wait, and Gurudev pointed at the very strong sankalpa for water—almost all of the pieces performed were somehow connected to water. The Master is like a wish-fulfilling tree. It is important what sankalpas we take in his presence as nature would offer its full support for it! His love for nature is extraordinary. Rejuvenating rivers, planting millions of saplings, cleaning rivers and lakes, preserving indigenous seed varieties, caring for animals—his efforts have been consistent and persistent. People have often asked him if he ever gets tired and he replies, 'Does the sun ever get tired of shining or the river of flowing? When one does what is in one's nature, one doesn't get tired or stressed.'

There was a song that was composed for the WCF in Berlin. Gurudev had contributed some verses to the song— 'Can you hear my call? The call of ancient love ...' That was how I exactly felt, standing amid the thousands who had heard him and answered his call. One is familiar with the phenomenon of love at first sight. As it happens, most often the feeling decreases, decays and, sometimes, turns to hatred or indifference. Gurudev says, 'When the same love becomes a tree nurtured by the manure of knowledge, it becomes ancient love that goes from lifetime to lifetime, and is part of our own consciousness. You are not limited by your present body, your present name or form and the relationships around you. You may not know your past or your ancientness. But knowing that you are ancient, that is enough!'

I feel so fortunate to experience this ancient connection, moving from one lifetime to another, answering its call. Time and again, this call has brought together an ocean of humanity to celebrate and honour life. As mentioned before, in the early 1990s, when Gurudev conceptualized the primary sketch of our meditation hall, Rajshree Patel, one of Art of Living's early instructors, said, 'It looks like a wedding cake to me.' Gurudev smiled and pointed to the top part of the sketch and said, 'I will be seated here, and there will be thousands of people all the way up to the main gate.' He gestured as if the structure were visible to him. 'There will be big screens through which people will see me.' LED screens were unknown at that time, so I imagined projector screens like those in movie halls. He went on to say, 'We will conduct a big programme and the whole world will be a part of it. We will have art and cultural programmes from every part of the world.' In the early days, thirty people was the usual number for a satsang; 300 people were a big number; 3000 people were considered huge; and 30,000 would have been a dream come true. Only Gurudev saw three million people.

'Good people will come together. Pearls just need a string to hold them together,' said Gurudev at our Silver jubilee celebrations attended by about 2.5 million people. I had never seen so many dignitaries together on a single platform ever before. Former prime ministers, presidents, over a thousand religious leaders from every faith, artists and musicians— the range of activities that was organized was phenomenal. How could one even control or coordinate anything of this magnitude! It was a glimpse of all the dynamism that existed around us. The distinguished speakers shared their thoughts and expressed their amazement at the scale of the event. It was a task ensuring that each of them got an opportunity to speak. And only after the three-day event did we realize that Gurudev did not get an opportunity to speak at all! But he did lead meditations on all three days, and it was an unparalleled experience sitting with 2.5 million minds that were dissolving together.

A group of villagers from the state of Uttar Pradesh, India, who had never ventured outside their hometowns earlier, travelled all the way to Bangalore carrying 120 kilos of ghee as an offering for Gurudev's mahayagya (the Silver Jubilee itself was considered a yagya). They drew the parallel of the squirrel trying to help Lord Rama build a bridge across the ocean. The night before the event, Gurudev had come over to inspect the stage and the preparations. While he was on stage, a labourer shyly approached him and handed over 5000 rupees as an offering. It must have been his savings from several months of hard work. Gurudev just took a hundred rupees from him and returned the rest saying that the feeling and intention to contribute were more important than the money itself. Drivers, vegetable vendors, farmers, every person contributed as much as they could for the event as if it were a special occasion at their own home.

Airports and railway stations were flooded with people carrying flags of their respective countries, brimming with elation and bursting with the festive spirit. They were all welcomed and accommodated at the homes of Art of Living volunteers across Bangalore. Imagine travelling to another country with no idea of where to stay! For our volunteers, the idea of a family extended far beyond the small circle of their brothers, sisters, relatives or friends. I remember the times when our mother would be confronted by people who would say, 'Your son has become a sanyasi and is leaving the family', and she would reply, 'No, he has not left the family but has made the whole world my family!'

The ashram was lively and the sole focus of the volunteers was to take care of everyone. Everybody acted as a host and nobody was treated as a guest. For the whole week, as far as the eye could see, there were people everywhere. Temporary structures were set up overnight and got filled even as they were coming up! Estonians, South Africans, Argentinians, Mongolians, Canadians and Israelis cut vegetables together and cleaned up together, rubbing shoulders with each other. At the event, they all came in their national costumes waving the flags that they carried along with them. Instructions were given to the people to take the position of the Bhastrika pranayama. All the 2.5 million people inhaled and exhaled in one breath. There was no separation between the air that we breathed in and breathed out. The space which contained the air contained us, and we were one with each other. Basking in this feeling of connectedness, I returned home.

As I got ready for breakfast the next morning, I received news that Pitaji was not allowed to come on stage as the new volunteers were unaware of who he was. So he decided he would instead watch the programme on television. The next day, Pitaji returned to Urugahalli, the village where he was working on women empowerment projects. Gurudev asked me to go bring him back. I explained to Pitaji that there was so much confusion at the venue because of the high security measures there. Somehow I was able to convince him and he came back with me to the ashram. Gurudev took Pitaji to the grounds in a helicopter and made him sit beside him on the stage. A.P.J. Abdul Kalam, the then president of India, arrived a few minutes later, and Gurudev requested Pitaji to welcome him. My father had always been a staunch supporter of the Congress party and was deeply respectful of statesmen. He was proud that his son had given him the opportunity to meet, receive and honour the president of India. I was remembering our Amma a lot at the moment. She would have felt very proud.

The same night, a few devotees received warning phone calls that there could be a terror attack at the venue. In the morning, Gurudev was so busy receiving dignitaries and attending to the needs of the programme that I was not sure if I should discuss the matter with him. Hours went by in a flash and the event was about to start. The grounds were filled with people, the stage with artists, dignitaries and volunteers, and my mind with concern. I prayed and knew for sure that my prayers would be answered. At that moment, Gurudev started the programme by chanting 'Om'. Instantly, all energies were channelized as the primordial sound resonated across the grounds. The second 'Om' followed. When I opened my eyes after the third 'Om', the sun was setting and everything around me was glowing. My eyes searched for Gurudev. When I saw him, he had a golden aura about him, and it looked as if the Jain and the Buddhist monks at the venue had halos around them. In fact, every man, woman and child who were part of the programme were glowing. The verses of the Gayatri Mantra resonated within me. I have always experienced the deity as a golden orb of light, but today it seemed as if she had descended to the earth on the Master's invitation. The light emanating from Gurudev was illuminating every person around him, encapsulating the entire radius of the grounds. I forgot about the terror threat after my ethereal experience and went back home feeling light. Only that, when I woke up the next day, the memory came bouncing back. But then, it was already in the past.

Ten years later, in March 2016, the stage was set once again for the biggest cultural olympics in history! The memory of the silver jubilee was still alive, but here I was again at another mammoth event. This time the stage was a floating structure and was spread across seven acres in New Delhi on the banks of River Yamuna. It was difficult to see where one end of the stage started or where it ended. There were 35,000 artists on stage! The WCF was scheduled for the evening, but people started arriving several hours before time. But just as the programme was about to begin, the sky darkened and it began to rain heavily. The entire land mass turned into slush. There were not enough umbrellas for everyone. VIPs, villagers, children and artists, everyone was drenched and it was turning chilly as well. Millions of eyes looked up at the sky in askance. The rain stopped for a few moments but came back with twice the force, this time accompanied by hail stones. Musical instruments were getting wet and it was getting windy too. I looked around for Gurudev. It was pointless trying to find anybody amid a sea of people, that too during the rain, but it was difficult not to spot him. He got up from his seat and started walking across the pavilion towards where the seating arrangement for the prime minister was made. Volunteers rushed with umbrellas but he waved them away. He walked alone in the pouring rain and was soaked from head to toe. When he reached the side stage, the sky relented and a spectacular rainbow arched across the area. I was thinking of all the people standing their ground and praying. One might have expected at least a partial exodus, but more people were flowing in now, having to cross huge puddles of slippery mud. Come rain or shine, no one was going to miss the moment. The rains caused the giant LED screens to short circuit. I looked again at my Guru, who was holding sway over 3.75 million minds at that moment.

The programme began with Vedic invocations, drum beats, dances and an orchestra of a thousand instruments. The performers came from across the world, and the performances were flawless even though the artists had practised and coordinated primarily via Skype. I could feel something imperceptible happening despite all the chaos and activity on the stage. My mind was still while I received and attended to the dignitaries and enjoyed the spectacular performances. I was told that the performances looked remarkable, but on stage, the order of programmes kept changing every moment. Perhaps it was all planned that way. Three hours passed by in a jiffy.

While most of the important leaders were in attendance for the event, there was also strong resistance from many, including some political and spiritual organizations. Taxi and autorickshaw drivers were apparently bribed to not service the attendees; deliberate traffic jams were created en route to the event; and baseless accusations were made and cases filed in the court for environmental damage. We had visited the site a year before when Gurudev decided that the event would be held there. The place was reeking. When one could not even stand there for five minutes, how could anyone hold a three-day event? Gurudev said, 'It is our job to remove bad odours and spread fragrance.' The place had been a dump yard for several years, and it was cleared painstakingly by the volunteers. A few environmental reports had classified the Yamuna as a dead river. The cleansing efforts removed over 500 tonnes of garbage from surrounding areas and the river bed. The efforts reached a point where birds and animals could once again start visiting the area after decades. Still, heavy fines were imposed for causing environmental damage. The media sensationalized a historic event that brought together people from 155 countries. Whether the coverage was positive or not, the whole country came to know of it. Millions followed the event online. I was reminded of the entire armies that came to fight against one Sage Vasistha. He placed his brahmadanda in front of his ashram and sat down to meditate. The armies could do nothing.

Even on the second day, just as the programmes were about to commence, thunderous clouds gathered above the venue. Gurudev's eyes were on the sky, and my eyes on him. He signalled me to start the Guru puja. Strong winds started blowing and the chandeliers at the venue started swaying rather dangerously. I closed my eyes and started the puja. Over 15,000 pundits joined me and sacred hymns started reverberating across the area. Thoughts are like clouds that roll in—they come and go. The sky is a witness. As millions of people gathered on the banks of the Yamuna with the sacred hymns flowing and cosmic connections being made, the ominous clouds cleared out of the sky and our minds.

Gurudev remarked, 'From regional to national and then to universal consciousness, this is the growth that the human race is looking for. We have gathered here from different countries, we speak many different languages, and follow different faiths with the intention of bringing love and harmony in the world. When there is tension between communities and conflict between religions, man becomes disturbed and is lost. In such an environment, people try this and that and wander here and there to no avail. When millions of people around the world are stressed and disturbed, a single cry arises from the hearts of everyone: *Sarve jana sukhino bhavantu*—let everyone be happy. This intention is already in every heart, it only needs to unfold a little.'

The meditation that he led was marked by absolute silence. It is so difficult to maintain silence with just ten people in a room, but here there were millions. Later, while glancing at the pictures of the event, I saw that even small children maintained utmost discipline and meditated! After the event concluded, the venue was cleaned spotless and was green within a week. Various enquiries commissioned by the government showed that there was no soil compaction in the river bed as alleged. Many people I met and knew were grateful to Gurudev for giving them an opportunity to be a part of the magnificent event. Gurudev, in turn, wrote a note to everyone:

> I know not how to thank you,
> For you are truly a part of me.
> With me every moment,
> Together at every step are we
>
> On the inner stage
> Consciousness dances unfazed
> Formless takes form,
> The cosmic creation stands amazed.
>
> Stage and dancer merge into one.
> So do the seer and the scenery
> The speaker and the audience,
> The Master and the devotee.
>
> This is the only truth,
> The rest is maya's cover
> Whom to thank here,
> When there is no other.

EPILOGUE

PEOPLE EXPERIENCE THE ocean in multiple ways. Some enjoy the cool breeze and are satisfied. Others stroll along the beach and collect seashells. Some others wade through the waves, some prefer to swim, while some dive deep into the ocean to gather pearls. Whatever your desire is, the ocean does not judge you and exists to just serve you. The ocean never compels anyone to search for pearls. Similarly, a Guru is an ocean of knowledge, of deep love. He does not compel but is always available to anyone.

On 2 October 2016, a peace treaty signed between the Colombian government and the FARC was rejected in a popular referendum in the country with 50.2 per cent of the voters choosing to vote against the deal. The people felt that the treaty was letting the culprits off the hook. Life could take a turn at any moment, and one had to be alert. Circumstances may not be pleasant always, and many challenges come unannounced. Spirituality is all about how one deals with a situation. If one can accept the present moment as it is, it is always possible to find an amicable solution. To break out of the impasse, the FARC and our volunteers in Colombia reached out to Gurudev. How to convince the people of Colombia to accept the change? Gurudev appealed to the

FARC to win the hearts of the people. A programme was conducted for members of the FARC and the families of the victims to come together and discuss their misgivings. They were ready to forgive instead of punish. On Gurudev's advice, FARC members appeared on television, expressed their grief over the lives lost to violence, and offered public apologies, remembering the names of individual victims and requesting their families to give peace a chance.

A few weeks later, the treaty was approved in a new referendum albeit with a few revisions. There would be many ups and downs as we traverse our life's journey. Often we tend to question ourselves and everything around us. But real happiness occurs when one can turn these questions into occasions of wonderment. I can recollect many instances when my mind kept oscillating between considering Gurudev as my brother and my Guru. Whenever I am exposed to his discourses on wisdom, I often wonder, 'Is this really my brother?' I cannot explain the feeling, but there is a sense of an unbounded presence that is beyond the limitations of siblinghood. I am reminded of the words of Yashoda, the mother of Lord Krishna, in the Srimad Bhagavatam. She says, 'I know that he is my son, but it feels as if I have been trying to catch the wind with my pallu.' How is it even possible?

My Brother. My Guru. As the heart alternates between the two roles, 'my', which is a sense of belonging, remains the only constant. It is a subjective connection. The essence of life is to feel a personal connection with the divine, but I am happy that I could see beyond our familial relationship and recognize him as my Guru. Experiencing the Guru Principle is the most amazing thing that has happened in my life. It is the peak of life's experiences. Gurudev says, 'The enlightened one is not on the peak. Rather, the peak is beneath the enlightened. One who goes to the peak comes down, but the peak seeks the one who is stationed in the plateau of the inner space.'

The Sanskrit word sahodari, translated into English as 'sister', means the one who shares a womb with you. I often wonder how a womb could capture something so boundless. In his compassion, Gurudev chose to share that space with me. Even if he were to limit himself to a body, a tiny corner of my heart would still feel that limited connection. Infinity is real and intangible, but a Guru is both infinite and tangible. Each time I sense an expansion of space within me, my small identity vanishes and merges with infinity. Perhaps this is what surrendering oneself is all about. Traversing life's precious moments, remembering the divine in every breath, I surrender again and again. In my journey to eternity, every step that I take is a goal unto itself.